THE LEADERSHIP LIBRARY
VOLUME 5
LEARNING TO LEAD

THE LEADERSHIP LIBRARY

Volume

5

Learning to Lead

Bringing Out the Best in People

Fred Smith

Carol Stream, Illinois

WORD BOOKS
PUBLISHER
WACO, TEXAS

A DIVISION OF
WORD, INCORPORATED

LEARNING TO LEAD

Copyright © 1986 by Christianity Today, Inc.

A LEADERSHIP/Word Book. Copublished by Christianity Today, Inc. and Word, Inc. Distributed by Word Books.

Cover art by Joe Van Severen

Library of Congress Cataloging in Publication Data

Smith, Fred, 1915–
Learning to Lead.

(The Leadership Library; v. 5)
1. Christian leadership. 2. Pastoral theology.
I. Title. II. Series.
BV652.1.56   1986   254   85-28010
ISBN 0-917463-08-0

Printed in the United States of America

With grateful memories of
my pastor/father
and
his courageous wife—my mother

Bunyan Smith (1886–1959)
Amy Anderson Smith (1890 1983)

CONTENTS

FOREWORD

Fred Smith's thirteenth-floor office overlooks two Dallas freeways and, in the distance, Texas Stadium. On the wall opposite the window is a wooden plaque that reads:

LORD, FILL MY MOUTH WITH WORTHWHILE STUFF,

AND NUDGE ME WHEN I'VE SAID ENOUGH.

For Fred Smith, that prayer has been answered time after time. As a communicator, Fred has a way of identifying the essence of an issue and speaking to it directly and pointedly. It's a skill he has worked hard to develop.

He once compared himself to a logger clearing a logjam: "The smart logger climbs a tall tree and locates the key log, blows it, and lets the stream do the rest. An amateur would start at the edge of the jam and move all the logs, eventually moving the key one. Both approaches work, but the 'essence' concept saves time and effort."

When it comes to effective leadership, Fred is equally succinct: "A leader is not a person who can do the work better than his followers; he is a person who can get his followers to do the work better than he can."

Fred is not easily described: a businessman, consultant, active Christian, and public speaker much in demand. When he was forty years old, he turned down the presidency of a national corporation so he could continue his broad involvement in business, education, lecturing, and church work. He has been a consultant to such corporations as Genesco, Mobil, and Caterpillar. He has served on more than twenty boards, including Youth for Christ and Christianity Today, Inc., but he no longer accepts such invitations, because "at this stage of my life, I'm more dedicated to individuals than to institutions."

The son of a pastor, he understands life in the parsonage; as a contributing editor to LEADERSHIP, Fred has produced articles that subscribers consistently rank among the most helpful. Readers don't always agree with him, but they appreciate his keen edge that cuts through the undergrowth.

As LEADERSHIP editors, Terry Muck, Dean Merrill, and I have considered it a privilege to work with Fred on this manuscript. Each of us has learned much as Fred talked through and we polished his thought-filled chapters.

His down-to-earth insights on *Learning to Lead* have been gained through years of experience. As such, this book is consistent with the vision of THE LEADERSHIP LIBRARY: to produce a continuing series of books that address the vital elements of church ministry with practical, proven ideas. In these pages, you'll see that Fred also remains faithful to yet another pledge he has framed and posted in his office:

I AM ONE AND ONLY ONE
I CANNOT DO EVERYTHING
BUT I CAN DO SOMETHING
WHAT I CAN DO I OUGHT TO DO
WHAT I OUGHT TO DO
BY THE GRACE OF GOD I WILL DO

—Marshall B. Shelley
Senior Editor, LEADERSHIP

Learning to Lead

O N E

LEADING: A PERSONAL THING

Leaders get out in front and stay there by raising the standards by which they judge themselves—and by which they are willing to be judged.

Not long ago, I met with twenty-three pastors who by almost any standard would be considered successful. They were men of God. They had either built large churches from small beginnings or had taken over growing churches and continued the growth. They were men of good spirit, dedication, and humility, and as I sat there listening, I noticed they were quick to give God the glory. Too quick, it seemed to me. I had to chide them.

"I'm a little tired of hearing you talk about God's blessing," I said. "If I took you twenty-three men and put you in twenty-three different towns, chances are the same thing would happen all over again."

Why? Because they know how to build churches, they're motivated to do it, and they know how to get people to follow them.

Does that sound unspiritual? I'm not discounting the power of God in the success of a ministry, but neither can we dismiss the importance of good leadership.

Recently, I had lunch with a young pastor from a small church who was wondering why things weren't going as well for him as for more successful pastors. He told of going to them and asking how they had built their churches.

"God has blessed us," they replied.

In all sincerity, my young friend wondered why God wasn't blessing his church. Was there some spiritual deficiency? Should he spend even more time in prayer and Bible study? Or should he get out of the ministry? Was he the reason God's blessing was withheld? "I feel so anemic," he said.

"You want to know the truth?" I asked.

"Yes."

"Those pastors lied to you." At least, they had not told the whole truth. I pointed out that God *alone* had not built those churches. I told him about chiding the twenty-three pastors for crediting God with their churches' growth when part of the reason was simply their strong leadership.

"You know," he said, "I could believe that."

He then went on to say, "I really don't have any background for running a church. During seminary I worked as a grocery store clerk, and everything was very structured. Then I worked on a church staff, and I was told what to do. I never will forget my first morning as pastor of this church when I woke up and realized there wasn't anybody to tell me what to do. I could loaf or I could work.

"That's where I need help. What are the things you put your attention on? What comes first, and what comes second?"

My heart went out to him. He was deeply spiritual—more of a man of God than most. But he lacked an understanding of leadership. And leadership is a subject that has fascinated me ever since childhood.

Leadership: More Than a Position

As the son of a preacher, I noticed a curious thing growing up: People in church leadership positions didn't necessarily know how to lead.

My father pastored a number of small churches in Alabama, Kentucky, and Tennessee. Unfortunately, many of the people were small too. In those churches, factory workers who ran plant machinery by day came to board meetings at night and tried to become executives. It didn't work. Even in my early teens, I could sense the ineptness.

As employees, they had no experience in good management, and they were incapable of offering anything better for the church. They assumed places of leadership without having leadership training. I watched day laborers with warped ideas of what it meant to be the boss become absolute dictators in the church.

One of these men would suddenly find himself chairman of the board. He did not know a thing about organization, future planning, human dynamics, or vision. He didn't practice leadership in his job, or even in his own family. Yet suddenly he would become a religious mini-mogul.

What was worse, these people rarely recognized their lack of ability. They assumed leadership was a *position* when in fact it is a *function*. Leadership is not a title that grants you license to force others to knuckle under; it's a skill you perform, a service you render for the whole group.

I saw my father as a genuine man of God. His longest stay was in a small church in the cotton mill section in Nashville. He became something of a padre of the slums. He had no fear of walking through the dangerous parts of the city. In the first place, he was an extremely strong man, powerfully built. He'd been a blacksmith when he was young, and I don't think anyone would have touched him. In the second place, however, he was revered by many in the neighborhood as a godly man. It does something to a son when you know your father is held in that kind of reverence.

But he was not a politician, nor was he gifted organizationally. When he would be outmaneuvered or put down by the power brokers in the church, I wondered, *Where's God in this? If we're supposed to be serving God and God is supposed to take care of us, then why is the rich guy (or vocal guy or angry guy) able to run us off? Are these people more powerful than God?*

Dad was a people person, not a natural manager. He would let things take their course without offering much structure. As a result, he struggled throughout his ministry.

My mother was the manager; she was a very well-organized person, and I admired organization even then. She saved us from starvation—stretching the $125 a month my father made so it could feed seven people. I could see these lay people did not have the leadership and management skills my mother did.

These experiences convinced me of the value of an orderly way of doing things. I grew up wanting to become a leader—not just to occupy a position of leadership, but to perform capably. I saw this as a valuable part of ministry.

Three Legacies

After forty years in the business world, I can still see my father's influence in me. He's one reason for this book. He taught me many things, but three of the lessons especially are reflected in these pages.

First, Dad was a stickler for integrity. At home he was a strict disciplinarian. Most preachers' kids grow up as somewhat public figures, and my father constantly reminded my brothers and me that we had to be examples. As far back as I can remember, we had to be at church (on time!); we had to have our Sunday school lesson complete; we had to be kids who would reflect respect and validate Dad's ministry.

Dad was very specific: He told us Scripture said he had no right to be a pastor if his family was not "in submission." He said if any of us five boys began living in a way that dishonored the church and Christ, he would resign. It was a threat, but we knew he meant it. And we all knew that preaching was his whole life.

While that was a heavy burden, it made us keenly responsible, right from the beginning. While I resented certain things—having to dress neatly, for instance—the situation never drove me to be rebellious. We always saw clearly the reason Dad wanted these things. And that is a tribute to him.

I inherited my father's admiration for integrity, and I trust that passion is bequeathed on these pages.

Second, I learned to appreciate the spiritual side of life.

Most pastors' homes, I suspect, face squarely the constant juxtaposition of the spiritual and the material. Ours certainly did. Our home existed for the spiritual welfare of the church. I never even heard business discussed, for example, until I left home at age twenty-one. I had to gain all my business knowledge as an adult (and felt envious of the children of executives—just as those who come to Christ later in life often envied us preachers' kids for our Bible knowledge).

And yet, the material side of life was a continual struggle. When I asked why our family didn't eat in restaurants more often, Dad would say, "A minister's family makes certain sacrifices. Eating out is not bad. But our family is centered on spiritual things, not material." We always knew heaven was as real to Mom and Dad as earth. And I continue to believe that material gain does not make a person wealthy.

He taught me another lesson, however, which became one reason I've been writing for pastors. Dad taught all of us that whenever you have knowledge that could help other people, you're supposed to share it. When the opportunity to write for LEADERSHIP arose five years ago, I wanted to offer what I could.

One of the rewards has been receiving letters such as the following, which arrived recently.

Dear Mr. Smith,

I'm the pastor of a small country church outside of Dallas, and so many times I get confused. The needs are so great, and I am so feeble in my answers. Your writings in LEADERSHIP *and* You and Your Network *have been such a clarifying force.*

I'm in my thirties with a wife and two children, the church is successful to many of my peers and so am I. But, Mr. Smith, I'm desperately hungry for more. I want to be a man of God. That's enough challenge for one life alone. I am also confused about desires I have to obtain security and luxuries for my family. They seem to conflict. I don't know whether to passively wait on God in these areas or to seek my own success. I know you're a busy man, but I could use some insight.

Shortly afterward, we had a very productive visit.

I don't have all the answers for pastors. They face many struggles I have not. But perhaps my forty years of experience in business, decision making, and leadership roles can be helpful in identifying some of the elements of leading, of bringing out the best in people.

This is not an exhaustive treatment of the broad topic of "leadership." This is hopefully the essence, a foundation from which the rest can be learned.

If a young pastor, like the one mentioned at the beginning of this chapter, were to ask "What are the most important things to know about leadership and management?" and if we had the time, the rest of this book is what I would say.

T W O

WHAT LEADERS ARE

To embark successfully on a career involving leadership demands courage. Once a person has decided the part he wishes to play in life, and is assured he is doing the work for which he is best endowed, and is satisfied that he is filling a vital need, then he needs the courage to tackle the problems he must solve.

T he pastor of any church wears many hats. The smaller the church the more hats worn. Effectiveness is determined by how well they fit and whether the pastor is able to choose the appropriate hat for each responsibility.

For example, each pastor's hat rack includes that of preacher, pastor, administrator, counselor, and fund raiser, to name just a few.

One of the most important hats, however, is that of leader. Leadership is necessary for any church to grow and penetrate the community. Why? Because leadership is what enables an organization to bridge the chasm between where it is and where it should be. Crossing the Red Sea, passing through the desert, or facing any immediate difficulty, any group small or large requires leadership to make progress.

Of course, if the group isn't going anywhere, leadership isn't important. But is status quo a station stop on the Christian way?

It's like the story of the pastor in the black church who was preaching. "This church, like the crippled man, has got to get up and walk!"

And the people said, "That's right! Let it walk."

"This church," he continued, "like Elijah on Mount Carmel, has got to run!"

"Let it run, preacher!"

"This church has got to mount up on wings like eagles and fly!"

And they said, "Let it fly!"

But when the preacher said, "If it flies, it takes money!" the people shouted, "Let it walk."

Some churches, like this fictitious one, don't want leadership. They just want to be comfortable. They don't want to cross any chasms, to grow or penetrate. Leadership is what gets people moving.

Leadership Is
a Function, Not a Title

Some individuals think they are leaders when they are not.

One of my friends in industry was asked by his son, "Dad, what does it take to be a leader?"

The man spent an hour struggling to reply and finally in desperation gave the best definition I ever heard. "Son, all it takes to be a leader is to have somebody follow you."

That's all it takes: followers. If people are not following you, you are not a leader. You may have the title, but that's all.

A church can call you to be a pastor because *pastor* is a title. The call does not make you a leader. *Leader* is not a title but a role. You only become a leader by functioning as one.

I remember sitting once in a city park at "Soapbox Corner" where the eccentrics assembled to do their public speaking. One fellow had attracted a large crowd with his harangue, and I noticed another man walking around the back of the crowd, obviously mad, gesturing as he muttered to himself, "I came here to talk. I didn't come here to listen."

He was mad because people weren't listening to him. They had left him to listen to the other fellow. He felt appointed a talker, not a listener. But the crowd thought differently.

We communicate only when people listen. And unless people follow us, we're not leaders.

Often leaders *don't* have the title. In a manufacturing plant, I've known many leaders of employees who were not in management, nor did they have a union job. But by the very dint of their personality and experience, they had authority. They were natural leaders.

The major characteristic of a leader in an organization is the ability to turn subordinates into followers. People can be subordinates by definition—by placement on an organization chart or membership roll. But they alone decide to be followers.

A friend of mine who owned a sizable company tried to motivate his employees by fear. In such situations, what generally happens is that people work only when the boss is around. During a visit to that company, I discovered that if my friend would be gone for a week, very little got done except the day right before he came back. The word went around, "The boss is coming back." Everybody got busy and caught up, but it was a sloppy operation.

With good leadership, he could have been gone a month and the organization would have functioned well. He was not a leader; he was merely a boss.

Some people base their claim to leadership on "being called by God." But until they have followers, they are not leaders. You can claim God called you to be a father, but until you have a child, you are not actually a dad.

Spurgeon, in his lessons for young preachers, said, "Gentlemen, if you cannot preach, God did not call you to preach." We shouldn't apply that too tightly, but there is a truth here: God does not call you to head any group you can't lead. Plenty of other ministries don't require the gifts of leadership. God may have called you to be an assistant pastor, or a hospital chaplain, or a soul winner, or minister of visitation. But until you have the gift of leadership, you should wait before trying to lead.

Leading is a function, not a calling.

Leadership Is
Serving God, Not the Sheep

The right concept of leadership is vital. The theory is important. Some people distinguish between the theoretical and the practical, as if theory is not practical. But somebody cleared that up for me by saying, "Nothing is as practical as a correct theory."

Behind every practicality is a theory. Behind our moon shots was Einstein's relativity. Behind Edison was Faraday's theory of electricity. The concept comes first. And without a solid concept of leadership, you have a faulty leadership.

Currently one of the most popular concepts is "servant leadership." Properly understood, it's a helpful concept, but it has been terribly abused.

The Christian leader is primarily a servant of God, not a servant of the sheep. Many shepherds act as if they're servants of the sheep—a faulty concept. You are a servant of God, given to absolute obedience to what he says. To extend that to say you are the servant of each sheep is a fallacy.

Steve Brown, a pastor in Florida, said he nearly became neurotic when he used to think he worked *for* the church—because he had five hundred bosses. When your boss calls in the middle of the night to tell you something, you're supposed to do it. But if everybody in the church is your boss and you're their servant, you've got an absolutely intolerable position.

 Yes, you lead by serving, but the major expression of your service is your leadership.

Take, for instance, Lee Iacocca, a great leader. He is the servant of the Chrysler Corporation, but he doesn't ask the assembly line workers to decide where the company should go. He may solicit opinions, but Lee Iacocca doesn't ask the man on the machine to do anything except run the machine and run it well—and have faith in the company. Iacocca's servanthood is expressed by his leadership. If he were to quit leading, he would no longer be a trustworthy servant of Chrysler.

There are shepherds who constantly ask the sheep which way to go. If the pastor quits leading the sheep and starts following them, he is no longer a trustworthy shepherd.

In addition, a shepherd does not expect his compensation, blessing, or reward to come from the sheep. He expects it to come from the *owner* of the sheep. I don't know of any sheep that ever gathered around to applaud the shepherd. All they do is cause him trouble.

Sheep are the work. They're not the wage.　　　←

As leaders we have to say, "I'm going to get my ultimate strokes from God."

If we don't watch ourselves, we start manipulating things to get strokes from the sheep. If that happens, it's like what Jesus said about giving alms in public. God will say, "You've got your reward." You can lead with an eye on crowd approval, but if you lead primarily to be rewarded by the sheep, you're not going to be rewarded by the owner of the sheep.

This position is difficult for some pastors to accept because of their personality make-up. Some pastors prefer serving people. There's a certain ego satisfaction in doing menial things for other people. They justify it by saying, "I'm showing people I'm not above doing menial things," which is a prideful statement, when you think about it.

Leaders who say, "Anything you need, let me know. I'll cut your lawn. I'll drive the kids to school" are not serving God, nor are they offering their best to their people. They are failing to understand the doctrine of gifts. There's no point in a clumsy, all-thumbs person trying to be a carpenter. He might desire the servant role, but he isn't serving. If my gift is leading (as evidenced by my having followers), then my serving is leading.

Those who are by nature social workers have difficulty accepting leadership because they would rather be liked, respected, and appreciated. They would rather serve people than take them across chasms. Social work is a necessary function in our society, but that function is not leadership.

Leadership Is
Art, Not Science

There is no valid list of common denominators for leaders, no formula to follow. The ingredients vary in each situation. Sometimes, for instance, leaders must exhibit courage; other times, their decisions are so obvious no courage is required.

I could list several "Traits of a Leader," but it would be like giving a list of recipe ingredients without giving the amounts or mixing instructions. Most lists of leadership characteristics are simply intellectual exercises. You can go down the list and check them, but it doesn't mean you can put them together in a specific situation and be a leader.

For example, one of the greatest requirements of a leader is knowledge of human nature. But the application of that knowledge varies, depending on the activity. Napoleon was considered to be the greatest general because he was the master of human nature *in war*. This was the basis of his power. He knew how hard he could push, how far he could go, how much he could do with what he had. But that didn't mean he understood human nature in politics.

Winston Churchill showed tremendous leadership in the emergency of World War II. He tried to exert it afterwards, without the same success. Leadership is not a constant science; it is a delicate art.

Some people ask if leadership is innate or learned. I think it can be coached but never implanted. The great violinist Heifetz could be coached but not taught. In the early days, he could be taught notes and music and the technique of fingering and bowing. But later, as one great conductor said, "I can only tell him whether he is doing what he tells me he wants to do."

I don't believe you can make a leader out of someone without an innate gift of leadership, and leadership shows up in early years. Looking at a child three or four years old, you can see an emerging pattern of leading or following. That usually continues throughout life.

If a person has innate ability, circumstances and training will certainly bring it out. No three- or four-year-old is as great a leader as Lee Iacocca. The circumstances, the ego pressures, Ford Motor Company kicking him out—all these contributed to his concentration on leadership. He might have concentrated on being a literary figure or something else, but he concentrated on leading. Though I may not admire some individuals as persons, they still demand tremendous respect for their leadership abilities. And those abilities can be developed—in the right people.

At this point, you may be asking, "What should I do if I realize I'm a follower and not, at this point, a leader?"

Pastors in that position have to face themselves very firmly and ask, *Am I occupying a place of leadership without the talent?* They must then seek God's direction, and if it's financially possible, change positions. This would relieve a great deal of the present stress among pastors.

This does *not* mean getting out of the ministry! There are many places to *serve* in ministry. Much of denominational work, for instance, requires little personal leadership. Church staff positions. A ministry of visitation. Significant ministry can be done apart from the primary leadership role.

Can a pastor give the leadership function to a lay person?

Not while at the same time maintaining the image of himself as leader. It's a rare individual who can let someone else lead without occasionally trying to exert his own leadership by disrupting what the other person is doing.

This is what happens occasionally with pastors who don't have leadership qualities but want to "develop lay leadership." The lay leadership begins developing a following and scares the staff. Then, to prevent a coup, the staff begins to police, restrict, criticize, or organizationally obstruct. Pastors who are not leaders can get pushed into all kinds of dangerous manipulations, especially if their spouses want them to be assertive leaders.

Those who are not leaders will have to face that situation with integrity and follow the person who does have leadership. But then you have to admit you're not leading, and that is a difficult position for a pastor, as the job is currently defined.

Leadership Is
Both Material and Spiritual

Leaders are forced to relate to money. They need to understand its place and its power.

Money is not all there is to administration, though many times administration requires handling the budget and the accounting. Leaders get followers to support the cause, and that includes committing their money.

Leaders who refuse to admit their responsibility to raise money simply do not understand the full import of leadership. I've heard so many young people in ministry say, "I want to be involved in the ministry but not in the money." I can sympathize with the feeling. One of the first questions I'm going to ask when I see God is "Why did you tie ministry and money together?"

I've studied money for years. It is not just a medium of exchange. Money has a psychological power. We will delay almost anything—dreams, plans, family relations—for an opportunity to make money. Money is not only necessary for survival, but it seems to touch the center of our ego.

My experience on the boards of Christian organizations has shown me that much more ministry fails from lack of money than from lack of people to minister. One significant ministry was going out of business until it revamped its financial approach. The problem was not the ministry, which was healthy; the problem was a casual "God will provide" attitude toward money.

On the other hand, we must also avoid the dangers of greed and using questionable means to raise funds. Ministry is forfeited when people begin to think it is simply a money-raising scheme.

But leaders know that money and ministry are joined.

Leaders must accept responsibility to relate properly to money.

A Leader
Is Not the Cause

A true leader is committed to the cause, and does not become the cause.

Staying personally dedicated to the cause can become extremely difficult, particularly if the cause succeeds. A subtle change in thinking can overtake the leader of a successful ministry. He or she begins "needing" certain things to carry on the ministry—things that were not needed earlier.

In business, a request for a corporate jet is a sign that personal ego needs are infiltrating an executive's dedication to the company. In churches, perhaps the signs are less visible, but nevertheless leaders can begin thinking *What am I getting out of this?* Their focus on the cause has been diffused. They justify certain perks—denominational jobs, cruises, their picture in the paper—as "enhancing the ministry." They have more trouble distinguishing between themselves and the cause.

I admire Mother Teresa, who decided after winning the Nobel Prize that she would not go to accept any more recognition because it interfered with her work. She knew she was not in the business of accepting prizes; she was in the business of serving the poor of Calcutta. She maintained her dedication to the cause by refusing unrelated honors.

Most of us leaders have an emotional block occasionally. We need to return to the vision, restate it to ourselves, and rekindle the spark. We must ask, *What is my purpose? Am I satisfying my ego through this ministry or sacrificing my ego to it?*

Genuine leaders can say with Paul, "Follow me, as I follow Christ."

THREE
WHAT LEADERS DO

Captain Russell Grenfell, in The Bismarck Episode, *wrote: "Every ship's chief officer followed, roughly, this procedure: Analyse the situation as it is and the way in which it developed; visualize all the possibilities; assess them to determine probabilities; estimate the strength of the forces opposed and of our resources; decide upon a general plan; communicate it to those who should know; move to carry out the plan with economy of effort and material; be sure to calculate the chances of prolongation of action; and, most important, shoot at the proper target."*

We've seen that leadership demands a certain self-understanding. A grasp of what leaders *are* is a necessary foundation. Now come the tasks to be *done*. What are the most important responsibilities of a leader?

Maintain the Vision

David Rockefeller was once quoted as saying, "The number one function of the top executive is to establish the purpose of the organization." For pastors, too, perhaps the most important job is to articulate and maintain the church's vision.

Like the hub of a wheel, everything else grows out of this. Until the vision is established, you have all kinds of trouble. Scripture says, "Where there is no vision, the people perish." The New American Standard Version focuses on the *way* they perish—"Where there is no vision, the people are unrestrained." To be restrained, to be concentrated in purpose, is essential to accomplishment, and that is why the leader must define why this organization exists. What's its purpose?

A leader must personify the vision, be dedicated to it personally. For example, someone totally oriented to personal evangelism would have trouble projecting a vision for biblical scholarship. He wouldn't have time to be a scholar. The leader must put forward a vision he can be honest about.

Some leaders say, "What would this church like for me to say its purpose is? That's what I'll say . . . even though I don't agree with their statement and I'm not going to fulfill it."

I call these kinds of leaders "clouds without rain." In a parched land, they look promising. But they float on over, bringing only a shadow.

A vision has to be something both the congregation and the pastor can share. If the pastor has, for instance, a gift for pastoral visitation, the vision must include that emphasis. If the pastor is "growth-oriented," this should be included in the vision.

In maintaining the vision, here are several keys for leaders to keep in mind.

1. *Define it specifically.* In my view, nothing is properly defined until you write it down. Writing forces you to be specific; it takes the fuzz off your thinking.

When I was working for Maxey Jarman, anytime I was fuzzy in my thinking he would force me to write him a memo.

Once I said, "I can't write it."

He said, "The only reason you can't write it is because you don't know it. When you know it, you can write it."

Writing your purpose forces you to be disciplined in your thinking. You come to see the need for a vision broad enough that everything you do can be tied in. But the vision must also be focused enough that it sets some boundaries. The vision must state what you *will* do and what you *won't* do.

Take, for instance, a statement such as "We exist for the glory of God." That's great for somebody who wants to sound pious or doesn't want to be evaluated, but it isn't specific enough to help an organization make decisions about what ministries to emphasize.

2. *Express it so other people understand it.* A good statement of purpose is straightforward. It comes right to the point.

But it is more than a slogan or an image. Slogans are advertising. They're not really statements of vision or goal. An image is what you want people to believe you are, which may be a prostitution of the vision.

The vision can't be arrived at quickly. It calls for a great deal of objectivity. We have to know what we *can* do and what we feel *called* to do.

Some churches set a purpose "that our people know the Scripture." That's the central vision. Other churches focus on "realizing your potential." On the other hand, one of the fastest-growing churches in the South has Christian fellowship as its purpose. You hear such phrases as "It's neat to be a Christian." Everybody likes everybody, and you feel good when you come—the members are essentially consumers of friendship. Now you may argue about whether that's a proper basis for a church, but at least they are very clear about it.

Too many congregations have no purpose larger than to be an average church doing average things. That doesn't require great leadership. It requires what I call "maintenance leadership." It's not building for the future.

Some will object, "We don't want to be a narrow church. We want to have a wide ministry that encompasses many visions."

If you get too many and don't sort them into primary and secondary categories, you end up splintered. You're better off having a purpose that strongly attracts certain people than trying to be broad and shallow. When that happens, you really don't accomplish much at all. If you build a staff of four or five people, all of whom have different ideas about the purpose of church, you can't get the intensity, the drive you need. (Single focus is the strength of many parachurch organizations: They do one thing well. Those who spread too widely develop serious problems.)

If you don't focus sharply, you can also get into the confusion of doing one thing for the purpose of something else. Unfortunately, some "Bible studies" these days are mainly for the purpose of Christian social contact, a place to go park your Mercedes and have lunch.

3. Get both organizational and personal acceptance of the vision. Organizational acceptance means the majority will vote for the motion. A few churches will even back it unanimously. But voting for the organization to do something and voting to be personally involved are two different things. Leaders get people to commit themselves personally, not just to provide paid staff.

4. Repeat the purpose over and over. One very effective leader used this phrase in his vision setting: "Say it simply, boldly, and repeat it often." Any leader who doesn't constantly repeat the essence of the vision, perhaps in different words, will find the people straying. The purpose must be repeated and repeated and repeated because it gives meaning to the organization; it produces intensity and direction.

A church without a clear purpose can get involved in all sorts of tangential activities. People assume anything that brings people to the church building should be part of the program. If your purpose is "to get as many people through the doors as possible," anything that attracts is legitimate.

I met a young minister who had gotten sold on the "find a need and fill it" marketing idea. He wanted to use his church as a free employment agency for people who had been laid off. Certainly, people need jobs. If he was just looking for a need to fill, he'd found one. But I asked him, "Is that why you were called into the ministry—to find jobs for people?"

He allowed as how it wasn't, and he was able to focus the vision a bit more clearly after that.

When you have a clear vision, you view everything in light of it. Every once in a while you sit down and say, "Let's stack every activity in this church up against our purpose." That affects what a church does and how it spends its money in the future.

I spoke at a church not too long ago that claimed its vision was to be staunchly evangelistic. Yet they had fewer conversions in a year's time than they had staff members and officers. It made you wonder how long since they'd realigned their direction with their vision.

Gather Others around the Vision

The second function of a leader is to coagulate followers around the vision, not around himself.

This is where integrity comes in. If a leader coagulates followers around himself—I call that embezzlement. Using personal magnetism as a means of getting things done is, to me, manipulation.

For example, to say, "Would you do me a favor and teach this Sunday school class?" lacks integrity. We're not in the business of asking people to do personal favors for us; we want them to express their commitment to Christ. (Unless the person has a gift of teaching, he isn't doing *anybody* a favor by teaching a class. The people are usually doing *him* a favor by listening.) Genuine leadership gathers people around the purpose of the organization. Toward that end, leaders need to recognize several subtle dynamics.

Decisions are not commitments. The first is short-term, the second is long-term.

People decide short-term to work for a specific emphasis; long-term commitment is aimed at the ultimate purpose. Both are necessary. People committed only to the long-term vision and not to specific tasks will not accomplish much. The short-term commitment produces the activity. But that must be judged by the overall vision.

In evangelism, we see a lot of decisions. Billy Graham is right in talking at his crusades about *decisions*, not *commitments*. Decisions are often like New Year's resolutions. The leader's job is to move people from decision to commitment.

(I've observed that this is one difference between the spoken word and the written word. Speakers are most effective at bringing people to decisions, but generally it takes reading to bring people to commitment.)

Wise leaders know that when they get a decision, even a group decision, they have not gotten commitment. One of the worst mistakes a leader can make is getting a group to decide something they will not commit to. In the emotional moment of decision, you can assume they're committed, but things will fall apart.

Recognize the "driving wheels." There's a difference between people who provide the momentum in a group and those who go along for the ride. Wise leaders know that if they get the driving wheels committed, they will bring the others along. Without the commitment of the driving wheels, the organization moves unsteadily.

The best way to persuade the driving wheels is not with emotion but with comprehension. I first heard this from my close friend Jack Turpin, founder and president of Hallmark Electronics, in a speech on sustained excellence. He has no lasting respect for short-term excellence. "Anybody who can reach excellence should try to sustain it," he said. And he knows how hard that is.

He went on to say the only way people will perform excellently over the long term is if they fully comprehend what they're doing. A decision based on emotional fervor won't last. A fully comprehended commitment will.

This means leaders must be honest about the vision, the effort necessary, and reasons for expending it. We'll spend a whole chapter later discussing motivation versus manipulation, but for now I'll just say that lasting motivation is really *persuasion by comprehension.* If you have to hide the reasons you want a person to do something, you are probably manipulating, and you're not likely to get long-term commitment or sustained excellence.

The way to motivate the driving wheels is to say, "Do you agree this is something worth doing? If so, let's commit to it together."

Know when it's time to change the vision. Leaders know the situation does not hold still forever. In the church, one indication the vision needs adjustment is the demographic trend. If a congregation is maintaining its size, but the big percentage of new members are older, and the young people are leaving the church, it's losing the future leadership. Now, if you ask, "How are your numbers?" the pastor may say, "Holding steady," but it's getting to be an old-folks' home.

If the vision of the leadership is to start a retirement home, fine—they've got it made. But if not, they must do something to recenter the program. The goal is to make the interest of the church identical with the membership of the church.

Know the Value of Administration

Leadership and management are two different things. Many good leaders are not good administrators, and good managers are not aways leaders.

As president, Jimmy Carter was a better executive than he was a leader. He would read up to three hundred pages of reports before breakfast. He was one of our best-informed presidents, but he had trouble getting people to follow his leadership.

Ronald Reagan's strength has been leadership, not management. The press criticizes him because he often can't answer technical questions. But he is a leader. He's able to provide a vision for the organization, to get people feeling good about what's happening. People who don't like his leadership call him "the Great Communicator," suggesting that if a person is a talker he's not a thinker. But communication skills are key to leadership. Reagan delegates the administration.

Even if a leader is not strong in administration, he must recognize the absolute value it plays in the success of a nation—or a church. If you delegate it, you have to appreciate it, develop it, and then leave it alone. Oversupervision is the great sin of leaders against managers. The leader's task is to say, "Here's where we are, and there's where we ought to go." The administration's task is to determine how to get there.

As A. T. Cushman, the CEO of Sears, put it, "The art of administration is constant checking." He's so right. It's detail work. Managing takes a different set of skills than leading. You lead people, but you manage work.

Many pastors, of course, have to wear both hats. They are both leader and manager. In that case, they must recognize the distinct functions. Proclaiming vision from the pulpit is a separate skill from working effectively in a committee meeting. Proclamation is necessary for leadership, but it will probably be counterproductive in a committee meeting.

Choose a Style of Leadership

Since there are different ways to lead, it's important to make a very clear selection. Unfortunately, great numbers of people try to be Mr. In-Between. They refuse to select any one chair and end up sitting on the floor. The eclectic approach doesn't work.

Followers have an amazing ability to accommodate themselves to leadership styles. They want to "please the boss." But if the style is constantly changing, they withdraw, become inactive.

They will make *gradual* adjustments so long as they don't have to make *major* adjustments. If you will select your style, implement it, and stay consistent, you can almost use any style you want.

Here are some typical styles of leadership:

1. *The benevolent dictator.* I spoke recently to a group of young pastors who were very interested in seeing their churches grow. When I described the traits of a benevolent dictator, they immediately said, "That's who we are. We know where we're going. We know what we want people to do to help us get there. Yes, we want to be pleasant about it, but we think the way we're headed is right, and we really are not interested in other people's ideas for this church." They were interested in results, a great many of which could be expressed numerically (size of church, size of budget, growth rate).

I have occasionally run into preachers who were *tyrannical* dictators, but these weed themselves out pretty quickly. They develop what has to be called a cult. Even though it may be theologically sound, it is still a personal cult.

Tyrannical dictators rarely last in any organization. Their very meanness undermines them. By operating from a motivation of fear, they sow the seeds of rebellion, which erupt only when the people sense weakness. That, of course, is the very time the leader can't afford to have a rebellion. That's why tyrants don't last.

But the *benevolent* dictator is a common leadership form among pastors.

2. *The one-man operator.* Actually, this is more often a one-*couple* operation that runs the church like a mom-and-pop grocery store. Mom plays the organ, heads the missionary society, and makes calls with Dad, who does the preaching, the greeting, the supervising, and even the grass cutting. If they have children, the kids work in the choir or the Sunday school, and it's a family business.

A great many churches are like this. Many of them are small, of course, but some of them grow to be sizable, depending on the energy and talent of the pastor. As the church grows beyond what one man or family can do, it starts to wilt. Somebody else's Sunday school class starts to grow, and that's threatening to the pastor, so along comes a new policy that no class will have more than ten students. . . .

If this kind of church is located in a growing suburb, it may expand simply because of its environment, in which case the one-man operator may have to move on because he just can't keep his arms around it all.

3. *The team player.* Think about a football quarterback. He listens to everybody. He has a coach, but he knows his responsibility to call the play in a given number of seconds.

I saw an interview with Jim Zorn when he was still with the Seattle Seahawks, a couple of years after he had lost his number-one quarterback position to Dave Krieg. He said, "Football is a team sport, and if Dave Krieg can get more wins for this team than I can, then he should be the quarterback, and I will back him up. I will support him. I will watch every play and try to see things he can't see. I'll talk to him. We'll be friends. And I will support the coaches' decision to make him the quarterback."

The interviewer noted that this kind of attitude resulted from Jim Zorn's vibrant Christian faith. It was a great testimony.

In the church, I think the team philosophy ought to be common practice. If somebody else can do a job better than I can, I want him to do it. A true spiritual quarterback plays for the good of the team and isn't just trying to be a star; he's trying to win the objective for which the organization exists.

Now a dictator can't become a quarterback/team player any more than he can fly. He may adopt the jargon, but his style will remain untouched. I have to say this: I've seen limited success in people trying to change their style. For some reason adults develop reflexes, reasoning powers, and success patterns that seem to lock them in.

I tend to be a team player, and when I was forty years old, I was asked to be president of a national corporation. I met with the board and did some background study. They had had a dictator for the previous forty years. I turned the offer down, because I'm too lazy to be a dictator. If I had gone in there and called those executives together and said, "Make your own decision," they'd have looked at me and said, "Who? Us? We haven't made a decision in years." I would have hurt the organization. It would have taken me too long to change systems. What they needed was a young dictator whom people could respond to in a habitual sort of way.

Quarterbacks can't make decisions as quickly as dictators. A dictator is a broken-field runner, a punt returner. A team player is more of a Franco Harris, who keeps hitting the line consistently and making first downs. The two are different skills.

In a church, you can tell a quarterback by whether people feel their suggestions will be acted on. With a dictator, people do not feel individual responsibility. They may feel responsible *to him*, to give him information or even make suggestions, but they feel no personal responsibility for the organization. In a team operation, people feel responsible for the decisions.

4. *Leading by compromise.* I realize the word *compromise* has a very bad name. But life is not all black and white.

It is possible to lead by compromise. Lyndon Johnson was a master at it. He had a real sense in Congress of what was doable with the people he had, and he'd get people to bend. Many times this is wiser than stopping the total program for an all-out debate.

Now as president, I didn't think LBJ was as effective as he was in Congress, because his skills as a compromiser were not as suited. He was no longer among equals. He needed to lead more strongly.

A compromiser has a clever way of getting everybody to give something. I've seen a lot of people, both in industry and ministry, who are basically achievers of compromise. They don't go very fast. They don't generally go very far. But they go pleasantly. Rarely will you see an achiever of compromise split an organization. He'll find some way to bring the sides together.

5. *The consensus taker.* You can spot this person immediately, because he's always sending up balloons, raising a flag to see who salutes. If the balloon doesn't get shot down, this establishes his path for the future.

I don't want to gainsay the consensus-taker style. The Quakers, for example, use it effectively, but they have a clerk who states the sense of the meeting. Through this individual they accomplish leadership by consensus.

Ray Stedman, of course, has had an amazing system at Peninsula Bible Church in California of not doing anything until it's unanimous. He believes that is the scriptural way. On the other hand, I have known two churches just recently that ran into real trouble trying to institute that system. Ray's advantage in Palo Alto was that he got to set the pattern from the beginning of the church.

In such an atmosphere, a subconscious kind of politics

evolves over a number of years through which people edge along smoothly toward consensus. If you tried to institute this in a big Baptist church in my part of the country, it would be chaos. Everything would come to a screaming stop.

Whatever your leadership style, it is important to know who you are when you start employing people. If you're a dictator and hire some strong eager beavers, you're going to keep them only a short time—or else face a revolution in the organization. You want to hire people with hinges in their backs, and keep them oiled.

Similar forethought is important for the one-man operator, the team player, the achiever of compromise, and the consensus taker as well.

These, then, are some of the functions of leadership. The rest of this book deals with the areas where leadership and administration overlap—directing yourself, guiding your coworkers, and leading the congregation.

F O U R

PERSONAL DISCIPLINES

Leaders need to submit themselves to a stricter discipline than is expected of others. Those who are first in place must be first in merit.

Leadership, as we have seen, is both something you *are* and something you *do*. But effective leadership starts with character. When leaders fail, more often it is a result of a character flaw than lack of competence.

The aim of any Christian is to mature, to conform more and more to the image of Christ. This character development is especially important for leaders. And it's a process, not a plateau where we sit down to rest. Leaders who last don't stop growing; they continue to stretch themselves.

How do we discuss such an intangible personal quality? It's not impossible.

Growth must be seen as a whole. I wonder sometimes what we would look like if our mental, emotional, and spiritual aspects were as visible as our physical bodies. I suspect many of us would be distorted, misshapen, even grotesque. Some people develop their minds to the neglect of their social and emotional health. Others spend so much time studying the Bible that the rest of their lives are stunted.

Maturity is balanced growth. It's obviously difficult to measure, but here are several disciplines necessary for healthy growth. They can serve as a checklist to make sure we're maturing in all areas of life.

The Discipline of Freedom

Some pastors I know feel trapped—*I'm called by God to do this, but I don't like certain aspects of the job, and I don't feel free to change them.* This depresses them almost monthly.

They feel like slaves to the church, and slaves have very few options. They have emotional options, of course—they can be dedicated, enthusiastic, willing to use their best talents, or they can drag their feet and be insolent and difficult to get along with. But internal control is about the only control slaves have.

When feeling trapped, the key is to recognize you're serving the wrong master. Pastors, as I mentioned earlier, are to be slaves of Christ, not slaves of the church. This freedom to serve Christ alone, however, requires discipline. It comes with a price. All freedom does.

One of my wife's friend's once told her, "Your husband has more freedom to express his opinion than anybody I've ever met."

Mary Alice replied, "He pays a price for it." It's true. Mavericks must accept the price of being a maverick. So must pastors who want to be free to serve Christ alone. It's dishonest to want the benefits without paying the price.

A lot of people try to lease freedom instead of buying it. Leasing—trying in small ways to be something you're not in order to please people—is cheaper. It provides some breathing room. But by leasing, you never gain ultimate freedom. Freedom cannot be leased; it must be purchased, and you buy it at a price you do not set. You decide to have it, and then you pay whatever it costs. If you try to acquire it at your own price, you're leasing.

The price of freedom to serve Christ alone is often your willingness to be disliked. It may cost you your job. It may cost you relationships. You may be ostracized by your peers.

I was approached by an active Christian man about serving on the board of his organization. I said, "You don't want me, because I would see my responsibility to the organization and not to you. You couldn't count automatically on my vote." I was insisting on my freedom to discharge my responsibility.

He agreed I wasn't who he wanted for this position.

This desire for total freedom has to be tempered, however. Freedom is not irresponsibility. Freedom is an environment in which you discharge your responsibility. I believe one reason for America's productivity is that for the first time in history, responsible people have lived in an environment of freedom. The Puritan conscience was responsible—*you have a talent, you're responsible for it, and one day you'll stand before God and be judged.* When that was placed into an environment of freedom, it became tremendously productive.

We've seen this more recently with the boat people from Southeast Asia. They come into freedom with a sense of responsibility and the desire to get ahead, and they succeed.

One way I've discovered to remain responsible is by retaining my first love for Christ.

An executive friend and I were going on a business trip to Italy. He was a rock climber, very macho and profane. I said to myself, *This is going to be bad. He's not a believer. He's going to chase every skirt he can see.* But by the end of the trip, he had never looked at a woman or made a single suggestive comment. As we were seeing the sights, he kept saying, "I wish my wife could see this." Every day he wrote her. I realized he was totally in love with his wife, and it protected him from any other woman. He wasn't even tempted. By being a slave, totally committed to one person, he was totally free. I realized that only in total slavery do we have total freedom. I believe Paul experienced this as a "bond slave of Christ."

The more total we can make our commitment to Christ, the freer we are. We discipline our desires. We discipline our natural inclination for freedom without responsibility. Freedom carries certain restraints.

To be candid, however, only a few pastors have complete

freedom to serve Christ alone. Most have to balance their freedom with the constraints of the congregation and denomination. To be free, you have to be such a superior performer that others let you control the situation. Otherwise you settle for a lesser degree of freedom. If you have the biggest church in the denomination, the denominational leaders have more difficulty limiting your freedom. They need you more than you need them. That luxury, of course, comes only to a few.

The rest of us must settle for lesser degrees of freedom. As one of my pastor friends puts it, "You have to decide how much of your soul you're going to sell to stay in this work."

That's not as crass a statement as it sounds. Pragmatism has a certain integrity of its own. One of the first requirements of a leader is to stay a part of the community he's leading. Politicians say the number one requirement is getting elected. Even the most noble politicians can't represent their constituents' needs if they're not in office. Likewise, pastors may compromise a certain degree of their personal freedom, and do so with integrity, because they know the difference between long-term and short-term victory. Staying part of the community may be more important than insisting on their way over any given single issue.

Maybe an example from a different sphere will help. Even during an epidemic, a doctor has to sleep. Some individuals may die while he sleeps, but if he doesn't rest, he'll weaken himself and catch the disease, and more people will die while he's out sick. Therefore, while some may criticize the doctor for sleeping, the larger picture calls for a different view of the facts. So, too, pastors may have to balance their freedom in light of the total ministry. Only shortsighted people see each moral decision as an isolated incident. The discipline of freedom is remembering the long-term goal, not sacrificing it for the short-term satisfaction of winning a battle but alienating the congregation.

At the same time, we resist the temptation to do everything with one eye on congregational approval. Like my traveling companion in Italy, we have a prior commitment elsewhere, to Christ, that keeps us on course.

The Discipline of Emotions

Emotions can be hazardous to your leadership and productivity. I call certain feelings "blocking emotions" because they hinder performance.

Lust, for instance, is a blocking emotion. It blocks your relationship with God. David discovered that. It causes your relationship with your family to deteriorate. It tarnishes your self-respect. It also spoils your concentration, and the ability to concentrate is one of the greatest attributes of a leader. Intensity is like using a magnifying glass with the sun—you can burn a hole in something that way. Organizations are almost always in the hands of the intense. These people eventually take over.

Greed is another blocking emotion. It makes you rationalize all sorts of unreasonable things.

Another common blocking emotion, however, is what I call a "blue funk"—when you find yourself dragging mentally and emotionally. You can't lead effectively when you're depressed, and yet these moods are a recurring part of life.

The other night I came home tired. After dinner I sat down and went to sleep in the chair. I woke up two hours later good for nothing. In situations like this, I go through a series of temptations. One is to go to bed, but I know I don't need that much sleep. Another is to look in the refrigerator for something to eat, but I think, *I'm gaining weight now. I shouldn't eat that stuff.* Then another temptation is to start an argument with my wife. I don't feel good, so why should anybody else? But it's got to be a good righteous fight—"What? You're watching television again?" Or, "I worked real hard today. What did you do?" And suddenly two civilized people are into an uncivilized fight.

Other people can't bring you out of a blue funk; it takes self-discipline. Unless you find a way to interrupt the blue mood, you fritter away the evening waiting until you can justify going to bed. But you wake up the next morning feeling slightly guilty, unrefreshed, and the day is off to a bad start.

I have found a way to break that cycle. Blue funks generally happen when I do not have anything exciting to do after dinner. One of my disciplines is to try to have something planned immediately after dinner. I save little tasks I want to do or articles I want to read, to get me going during these down times. I enjoy little mechanical jobs, for instance. Often when I feel dull of mind, a little physical activity is a pick-me-up.

Certain kinds of reading also give me a lift. Sometimes I need a small amount of inspirational material, which I see as the printed equivalent of a Hershey bar—one is great, downing three would be a chore. I love to read Oswald Chambers's *My Utmost for His Highest*. He's always been illuminating to me. Not just the old inspirational froth that "you can do anything you want to do."

I enjoy short biographies. I'm not interested in four hundred pages on someone, but I do collect three- or four-page summaries of the lives of the great accomplishers. One of the great poets, Gamaliel Bradford, had vertigo so badly that he would even fall off chairs, but he never let it keep him from writing poetry. I begin to see that greatness comes only at a tremendous price. I'll read what Wagner wrote to Liszt, describing how wretched he felt and wondering if death wouldn't be preferable to living, but then he says, "But of course, that has nothing to do with the composing of my music." You see the intensity of an Einstein or a Newton; anything they observe gets put into a pattern. It's hard to remain lackadaisical and self-pitying when you meet people like that.

I've also found reviewing quotes helpful. A great quote is like a log coming along for a tired swimmer—it can help keep you afloat. I came across something Schubert wrote: "My music is the child of my gift and misery. Strangely enough the public seems to enjoy most the music I wrote at my most miserable times." I begin to see that the greats have produced in very difficult times. Or you might read of Tchaikovsky putting a sign on his gate: VISITING HOURS MONDAY AND TUESDAY BETWEEN 3 AND 5 P.M. OTHER TIMES PLEASE DO NOT RING. He was saying, "I'm a composer. This is how I'm going to bless the world—not by idle conversation." You see the discipline of the man. So when I find these kinds of good reading, I squirrel them away.

Another tool that works for me is the telephone. Two things I appreciate about the phone: (1) you don't have to answer it when it rings, and (2) you can call friends when you need help.

If you were out of gas, whom would you call? The service station. I know people who are like service stations—full of fuel. When I call them, all I have to say is "What's exciting today?" They're off and running. I don't have to say, "I'm overworked and depressed." I just have to ask what they're involved in, and just by listening to them, I get motivated. I've tried to develop a list of such people just for the down times.

If all else fails, however, and I'm still in a blue funk, I leave the house, go to a busy restaurant, have a cup of coffee, and watch people. I'm about half-dead when I'm in a funk, and that puts me among the living. I see something interesting. I see some kids who make me very proud of mine. I see people with problems I don't have. I begin to regain a sense of gratitude. I get a couple of thoughts about something I'm working on. I'm moving back toward normal.

Then I try to do something positive. Late one evening, I went to the all-night supermarket and bought Mary Alice a pot of white chrysanthemums. When I got home, she was still awake and appreciated even a small gift like this. (Anything that marks my return to civility is very much appreciated.) Seeing her happy, I went to my study and worked until 2 A.M. with a lot of zest.

After several hours of highly productive work, I can go to bed not requiring a lot of sleep because I've gotten energy from the positive experience.

Different stimuli work for different people, but the important thing is simply to find that first little push that starts you back—something you've wanted to accomplish, something to be grateful for, doing something for somebody else. Like a solenoid in a car, these acts require very little power, but they release the greater energy of the entire engine.

It helps to understand that your mind runs in cycles; there will be ups and downs. When you're in a blue funk, you think it will last forever, but it won't. During those valleys, you can find ways to pull yourself through. It takes discipline, however. The great temptation is not to do it, because for some perverse reason, most of us like being cantankerous at times. Effective leaders can't allow themselves that luxury too often.

The Discipline of Things

Leaders also have to come to terms, in a mature way, with possessions.

We live in a material world. That's the way God created it. There's nothing in the Christian faith that is antimaterial. The Garden of Eden was pretty lush. God gave wealth to Job. Joseph ended up in pretty comfortable circumstances. In fact, the early Christians opposed a heresy called Gnosticism, which claimed that material possessions were ungodly.

But if Christianity allows a place for the material, it is still *antimaterialistic.* When material things become a philosophy, a top priority, they become a stumbling block. Christians know material things are to be used for God's glory. When they become a measurement of success or value, they've become something God never intended.

What is my relation to things? Here are some questions to check if I'm growing toward maturity in this area.

Am I using my possessions and not just accumulating them?

In most families, heirlooms lend tradition and give us roots. I'm very proud of two pictures that hung on the living room wall when I was a small child. When I look at those pictures today, I become again a member of my family. Though my parents are dead, when I look at those pictures, they live again. My brothers are at home with me. Those pictures are material things, and yet I don't consider them materialistic things. They serve a healthy purpose.

Nor do I consider it materialistic to accumulate some things for our children to inherit. We recently bought six pieces of Cybis porcelain, some of the finest made. I was very conscious of the cost, but I also wanted some things we could pass to our children and they could pass to their children. These kinds of things tie the generations together.

Can I enjoy them and honestly thank God for them? I couldn't honestly thank God for a fifth of Jack Daniel, for instance. Maybe some people can, but I could not. Therefore it is not for me.

Am I able to share them? I love to go to a magnificent home of someone who has the gift of hospitality. I may never want such a home, but by sharing they've ministered to me.

I was traveling in Mexico one time and was offended to see, in a dusty, poverty-stricken town, a beautiful cathedral. I asked the priest how such a structure could be built amid such misery.

"Mr. Smith," he said. "The only thing of beauty these people can afford is what they have corporately. None of them alone can have anything beautiful, but together they can have this cathedral."

That changed my attitude. I wondered how I could have thought of taking it away from them. Yes, it could be knocked down, divided into rice and beans, and everyone could eat well for a year or so. But the rest of their lives would be impoverished because they didn't have something of beauty. By cooperation they created a treasure for all.

Am I able to give? Anytime I am less than generous with the things I have, I am less than Christian. Giving is the only antidote I know for greed. When we give things away, freely, without expecting in return, we help prevent ourselves from becoming possessed by possessions.

The Discipline of Recognition

It's important to get strokes, to be recognized for what we do well. The apostle Paul was constantly recognizing people for what they did. I'm always leery of an executive who says,

"Don't brag on your employees; they'll want a raise." There's something mean about that attitude. Recognition is important.

But we need discipline in deciding what kind of recognition we're going after. What kinds of strokes do we appreciate?

Woodrow Wilson said, "Many men are seduced by secondary success." Small successes prevent them from achieving big success. They're satisfied too easily.

I knew a runner in high school who set a national record, but he never followed through. He could have qualified for the Olympics, but he didn't want to pay the price. He had already succeeded.

Promotion is a form of recognition. But it takes more than a title to truly say, "I fill this position." Effective leaders are not satisfied once they've gained the title.

A pretty young girl said to her mother, "I get so tired of people saying I'm pretty. I wish they realized there was more to me than that." She wanted different recognition. She will have to augment the way she presents herself. She'll know she's succeeding if people begin to say, "She's not only pretty, she's smart." She will help develop the kind of recognition she prefers.

Some who are considered *smart* may want to develop *wisdom*. As people start commenting on their wisdom in handling life situations, they will know they're making progress.

A helpful exercise is to write down three words by which your friends describe you. And then write down three words you *would most like* to describe you. Then you can work on making those traits so prominent in your life that people can't keep from recognizing them.

Early in my life I chose seven qualities I wanted to develop. One, for instance, was objectivity; another was intellectual integrity. Then I got pictures of seven men I thought personified each of these traits and hung them on my wall as a continual reminder.

Leaders need to know what kind of recognition they're after, and can't be too easily satisfied.

The Discipline of Accomplishment

Closely related to recognition is accomplishment. I believe productivity—contributing to the community—is essential for mental and spiritual health. It is certainly true for leaders.

I was talking with one couple about their twenty-two-year-old son. They said, "He's not doing anything right now; he's waiting to find the will of God."

"Is he working?" I asked.

"No."

"Is he eating?"

"Yes."

I said, "Tell him he's violating the will of God right now. Scripture says if you don't work you don't eat."

I doubt he accepted that theological position, but work is scriptural; it connects us with the community. Exercising our gifts, contributing them to the body of Christ, is the primary source of our identity. Productivity is the rent we pay for our space on earth.

Obviously, there are different kinds of productivity. One can contribute to temporal things or eternal things. Christians should be involved with both.

Accomplishments come in two kinds: external and internal. Most of us concentrate on externals—our jobs, our acquisitions. But internal accomplishments are equally important.

Developing emotional stability, for instance, is a tremendous accomplishment. You don't do that overnight. People who learn to control their tongue, Scripture says, are "greater than he that taketh a city," which gives some indication how God compares internal accomplishment with external accomplishment.

Other people fight melancholia. Dr. Samuel Johnson said that when he was fifteen, he found he had a disease of the spirit. And yet he did so much, working around that handicap.

When you see people like Joni Eareckson living so productively despite her handicaps, or Ken Medema singing and writing music despite his blindness, you recognize that the internal accomplishments are as great as the external.

Leaders are aware of many different kinds of accomplishments and encourage them in themselves and in their followers.

The Discipline of Experiences

Life, like a river, is more easily navigated if it has numerous tributaries. The more sources, the deeper and broader it becomes.

People who are mentally healthy, according to a Menninger Clinic study, get their stimulation from a variety of sources, not just one or two. Sometimes Christians are tempted to be narrow—spending all their time talking only to Christian friends.

Frank Gaebelein, however, was an example of vigorous mental health. He was a Christian, a scholar, a mountain climber, a musician. He drew from varied experiences. To me, he's a great illustration of a mature Christian leader.

But in addition, I find it helpful to write down experiences, lest I forget them and lose their benefit. My wife has a wonderful practice of writing down every clever thing our grandchildren say. She now has a whole book of them. Along with an album of pictures, we have an album of family sayings. Thanks to her record, we can relive those moments and benefit from them again and again.

Leaders find that having, and recording, a wide variety of experiences is immensely helpful to their vitality.

The Discipline of Ideas

Small minds talk about things; average minds talk about people; great minds talk about ideas.

Minds grow as they grapple with ideas, and leaders monitor the kinds of ideas they are handling.

Are you interested in ideas? Are you fascinated by what you read in the paper beyond the crime stories and comics?

When Stephen Hawking talks about the black holes of space, or when Einstein writes about gravity as the distortion between time and space, does your horizon broaden with fascination?

I'm always pleased to meet some person of unusual mental attainment just to measure myself alongside him. Can I understand him? Can I keep up? I don't get envious or say, "Why didn't God give me that talent?" I'm just happy to know that people like that exist, and I can know them.

One of the measures of maturity is whether our ideas are growing, whether we're able to handle larger concepts, and whether we're comfortable with people who think.

The Discipline of Relationships

Relationships are obviously both the personal and professional concern of the leader.

First, your relationship to yourself. Jean Paul Sartre was once quoted as saying, "If you're lonely when you're alone, you're in poor company."

I visited a magnificent home built in a remote part of the Colorado Rockies. It was so quiet you could hear the paint drying on the wall. I thought to myself, *Only a person at peace with himself could own a home like this.* In that kind of magnificent quiet, you have time to be alone with yourself. And you'd have to be able to enjoy the company. You'd have to be satisfied with the way you are growing. You could not have your external success eating up your internal being.

That's one of the tests of maturity: the ability to be alone and at peace with yourself.

A second test deals with relationships with other people: *Am I increasingly able to spend time profitably with people who are different?* Immature individuals can't enjoy people who are different. They prefer people just like themselves. Maturity is being comfortable with diversity.

Finally, we must evaluate the development of our relationship with God. *Is my walk with God more comfortable? More intimate? More real?*

I had a friend who lost contact with God. The problem was this: instead of confessing, he was explaining. God is not very interested in our explanations. He knows why we do what we do. He doesn't need our rationalizing. But God is a marvelous listener to our confessions.

I've discovered I can explain things to God for years, but only when I get around to saying, *"Mea culpa*—I'm guilty," does my relationship with God begin to grow again. Relation grows out of confession.

Unless we can lead ourselves through these essential disciplines, we will have difficulty leading others. Having established this foundation, however, we can turn to another crucial battleground for leaders—the way we spend our time.

FIVE

AN EMERGENCY PLAN FOR SAVING TIME

No sluggard need aspire to leadership. There are passive persons who are content to go through life getting lifts from people; who wait until action is forced upon them. They are not of leadership material.

Most people spend time like they do money. They spend until suddenly they run short; then they seek a way to compensate.

The best approach, of course, is a disciplined lifestyle that prevents time (or money) from slipping away in the first place. This is what most time management books teach: Adopt a philosophy, implement it, and then maintain it as a way of life.

But most people will never be that disciplined. What they need is an emergency checklist to gain a few hours in the week—something to ease the frantic pace, to get them through the crunch.

Occasionally a worn-out pastor comes to me, and I say, "You're under the gun, aren't you? How much time would it take for you to catch up?"

He usually says something like "If I just had five more hours a week!" If he is working fifty hours a week, that's ten percent to loosen him up.

Here is a way to pick up five hours from any week you choose. It provides immediate and effective relief for those who are swamped. But it is for emergency use only. As in dieting or spending money, the long-range answer is a better lifestyle that doesn't require temporary bailouts. Mine is a battle plan, not a war plan. You shouldn't continue this emergency plan for longer than, say, four to six weeks.

Most pastors, however, can walk into a pulpit and say, "Folks, you're not going to see as much of me for the next six weeks as you have. I've gotten behind in some very important things I should be doing, because I've been doing other things that were needful. I'm going to need your understanding for the next month while I catch up."

People will identify with this and be very cooperative. Of course, if they hear that instead of working and praying, you're out playing golf, they will think you're pulling their leg. When you declare an emergency, it's got to be legitimate.

Here is my twenty-point checklist for saving time in emergencies.

1. *Clean off the desk.* To start the battle, sweep away everything you won't be using in the next six weeks. When I diet, I don't leave food lying around the house to tantalize me. Unfinished work tempts me, makes me want to look at it, pick it up, finish it. I feel guilty about it. So the first step is to clean off my desk.

I tell executives that the most productive week of their lives is the week before they go on vacation. They all laugh, because they know I'm exactly right. In that week they clear the decks, make decisions, delegate. They accomplish a lot because they quit messing around. If I'm going to quit messing around for a period of intense battle, I must remove from sight the intimidating stuff I'm not going to use.

2. *Stop reading the newspaper.* I can pick up three and one-half hours a week right there, and if I only need five hours, that's a pretty good start.

One of the finest Christian leaders I know analyzed his life and decided he was better off without a newspaper. But I also have a lawyer friend who won't leave his office without buying a paper for fear "someone may ask me if I've read something I haven't."

What a tremendous amount of reading time! How much easier to reply, "No, I didn't see that. What did it say?" The person can tell you in two or three minutes.

When not pressed for time, I can read the Sunday *New York Times* and get all the newspaper reading I need for the whole week. The thing I say to myself is *What am I getting out of the newspaper that's worth making my life frantic?*

The same principle applies to television. Break the habit of turning on the set without first checking the listings. Make TV watching a planned occurrence.

3. *Get up fifteen minutes earlier.* I do this more as an exercise of the will than to gain the extra minutes.

I know I can't lift a two-hundred-pound cement sack; it would overload my body. I must be just as careful not to overload my will. We often make resolutions with insufficient will power to carry them out. Then we get disillusioned and mad at ourselves when we fail. The truth is, we have weak wills.

Our wills may support getting up fifteen minutes earlier, but they won't support getting up an hour earlier. We say, "But I should be able to." That's fantasy. We've got to be objective about what kind of resolution we have.

Fifteen minutes each morning gives me an added hour and three quarters a week. Add that to the previous three and one-half hours, and the goal of five extra hours is already reached.

4. *Delay unnecessary reading.* I would postpone all reading that does not directly contribute to what I am doing during this emergency period.

Personally, I don't dare pick up a book at random. The other night I spent the whole evening in a fascinating book about the will, but if I were in an emergency period, I wouldn't dare pick it up. Otherwise, I'd be stuck with it. I won't starve myself for the rest of my life, but for a period of time I cannot permit myself to read randomly.

5. *Read only parts of books.* I'm surprised at how many people feel they *have* to read a book cover to cover.

If I'm in a hurry, I skim the table of contents, find the

subjects I need to know about immediately, and read those chapters. I'm a firm believer in not eating the whole pie. One piece gives plenty of ideas.

6. *Work on the majors only.* Some people have the unfortunate habit—and it is a habit—of listing each thing they have to do as if it were equal with all the others. I listened to a college group spend two hours debating a question that didn't deserve thirty minutes. But because they wanted consensus, and because everybody wanted to talk, they confused a major with a minor.

Not everything in life is of equal importance.

If I were a pastor, I would make a hierarchy of priorities to keep me from allowing emergencies to top the list. First I'd go with my personal spiritual vitality. What keeps me spiritually vital as a person? That's my number one job.

Second, how do I keep a good, productive relationship with my family? And what about my prayer life? My studying? These four priorities are usually the first to get shorted by people who have trouble with time. Perhaps these things are harder to evaluate than if I attended a Rotary meeting or solved an emergency.

For instance, if you belong to Kiwanis or some other civic group, skip one out of four meetings and take your wife to lunch instead. When people say, "I missed you," say, "You know, my wife is more important than the club." Don't go out calling. Make sure your family is the beneficiary on the days you give up the club. Wives appreciate that kind of statement.

During time battles, I ought to be able to write down the two, three, or four major things I simply cannot slight, and be sure only to work on them. These are my current majors, the items of greatest importance today. Everything else has to be pushed aside to work on the majors.

When the battle is over and I return to the routine war against time, I may have a completely different set of majors. I try to guide my life so my majors are consistently given importance.

7. *Make no radical changes.* I want to be very careful during

an emergency period not to make any radical shifts, because they require a lot of time to implement. The object of the battle plan is to pick up time, not to change. For example, I wouldn't try to review my habits for spending time. These are my reflexes, and it takes too much effort to change them. I wouldn't attempt to rework the organization or correct others' mistakes or get people mad at me and have to go back and apologize. I call these kinds of things "rework." I save the rework for the general war and concentrate on winning the present battle.

8. *Avoid the wood-hay-and-stubble activities.* Things that flatter my ego, satisfy my human ambition, make me liked— social affairs—are wood, hay, and stubble. If I have time for them, they're perfectly all right, but they are not eternal. And they can drain a lot of time.

I try to examine my life and ask, "What are the wood-hay-and-stubble activities?" Praying at the football game is not really a major thing if I'm pressed for time. It's a good ego boost. But if I'm in an emergency to recapture control of my time, I can't do it.

A pastor should list those church meetings he can stay away from comfortably. Lunch with the Women's Missionary Society every time it meets is not mandatory. There are many such meetings.

Under emergency procedures, I might even walk into a staff meeting and say, "Folks, I'm pressed for time. I'm going to have to ask your indulgence. Give me fifteen minutes to cover my subjects. You talk them out after I'm gone and then write me a memo on what our plan should be." Remember, that's for an emergency. They might let me do it for as long as six weeks, but I would be neglecting my responsibilities if I tried it every time. I have to decide what is wood, hay, and stubble at the present moment.

9. *Know my limitations.* A fellow called the other day who wanted to come by and talk. A part of Christian responsibility, I feel, is to see anybody who asks me—once. Beyond that, I am not bound, because it becomes an intellectual responsibil-

ity. If I can help him, I owe it to him; if I can't help him, I owe him nothing.

Because I was busy, I asked the fellow, "What do you want to see me about?"

When he told me, I knew I had no ability to help him at all. So I didn't see him. I didn't need to sit and talk to him thirty minutes, and then disappoint him. I told him very quickly by phone, without being brutal.

When I am pressed for time, I must pinpoint the counseling situations where I can uniquely help and then push the others to somebody else. But a lot of times, we will see someone out of curiosity (particularly if it's a woman) just to find out the story. An attractive, affluent woman recently asked me to spend a couple of lunches a month with her to mentor her. I said very frankly, "I cannot help you do what you want to do. What you need is real, but you need somebody besides me." We broke it off right there. There's no reason, just because she was pretty and had money, that I should spend time with her.

10. *Ask permission to say no.* When I need to decline something, I want to say no as simply and graciously as I can. When I ask for permission to decline, people generally give it to me. I don't say, "If you only knew how busy I am, you wouldn't ask!" I just say, "Let me ask a favor. May I say no?"

I do this with speaking invitations. I say, "You know, that would interfere with a section of time I really want to keep discretionary. If I agree to speak for you, it will come right in the middle of those two weeks. Do me a favor: let me say no." I handle it once, cleanly and clearly, and save a lot of time that way.

11. *Distinguish between information and relation.* Those who say to answer every letter when you receive it are missing a very important point. Mail and phone calls come in two kinds: information and relation. When I divide them up, I find most of my mail and calls are information. I can handle them once. But I don't want my habit to cause me to handle relational things that way.

If someone wants to know how much something costs, I can give the price now as easily as later. I won't handle informational letters twice.

But if somebody asks me a personal question in a counseling situation, I'm not going to say the first thing that pops into my mind. I ask myself, *How will this strike this person?* I have to think about relational questions, so during emergencies I postpone them if I can.

12. *Utilize a secretary for informational things.* I can hand-mark a whole stack of items where just information is needed, and my secretary knows how to handle them. She attaches a little note: "Mr. Smith is out of the office and wanted you to have this immediately. Here it is." People are glad to get it, and I don't have to touch it at all.

On the other hand, I don't ask my secretary to handle relational things. If there is anything that irritates me, it is for somebody else's secretary to call and say, "Mr. Jones would like to speak with you." Then I have to sit there and hold the line until he gets on. That's a relational matter, and he should be on the line when I pick up the phone.

13. *Deal only with the "driving wheels."* I mentioned in chapter 3 that every organization has some people whose thinking and action control everyone else's thinking and action. In order to save time during a period of emergency, I only deal with these driving wheels. They may not be the title people. But if we know our organizations, we can identify the driving wheels and the people I call the "idling gears." Many times a key secretary is the most important person in the whole organization. I never slight my relationship with her.

If I'm in a hurry, I spend time only with the people who make things happen, who form the opinions. I put the other relationships on hold for a while.

14. *Protect personal energy.* Since I work so much more efficiently when alert, I must protect my energy when time is scarce. One of the dangers of becoming harassed and time-pressured is that it cuts down energy and alertness. When

that happens, effectiveness suffers. So during an emergency period, I don't want to do anything that dissipates vital energy.

I find it very important during such a time to eat less and exercise more. If I had three wishes for pastor friends, it would be for more money, less food, and extra hours in the day. I can write articles about two of these, but pastors have to handle the food themselves. Cutting down on food, particularly sweets, is important. People eat sweets for sudden energy, but nearly all the research says they don't get that at all. Also, too much coffee interferes with sleep. We especially need to take care of our bodies in an emergency period.

My office is on the thirteenth floor. When I feel fuzzy, I go down to the eighth floor and climb the steps back up. It takes about two or three minutes, and by the time I get back I'm breathing hard, taking in a lot of oxygen. I don't attempt a cross-country run, but a little exercise revitalizes me. I can increase my energy and work a little longer because of it.

But I must also remember not to try to accomplish more by overworking. What I can do in fifteen hours is not three times what I can accomplish in five. Industrial research has shown that if employees work too long in a week, their productivity goes down the last several hours. A person has only a certain number of productive hours. I find I can work productively about ten hours a day. I can't handle twelve hours, so I shouldn't try.

15. *Schedule work according to productive hours.* For me, the first few hours of the day are worth more than all the rest. I can accomplish more getting up at five and working till seven than I can in any other four hours. So I schedule the really creative, productive things for those early hours. If I don't, I end up postponing work all week and patching together a last-minute job that looks exactly like it.

16. *Compile a list of second-wind jobs.* These actually refresh me. If I had to read the *Wall Street Journal* right after lunch, I'd be sound asleep in fifteen minutes. So I like to do something exciting that I've really been waiting to work on—jobs that

give me my second wind. They increase my utilization of time. Many times I'll call a friend after lunch and just sit and talk. By the time I get through with the conversation, I'm higher than a kite.

If I don't have anything exciting to do, I will do something routine. For example, I always walk through the plant after lunch because it is hard to fall asleep on my feet. Maybe I'll get my hair cut or go to the bank. But if I'm in an emergency and must shorten those downtimes, then I will use a job from my list. Second-wind jobs kill downtime and get me going.

17. *Discipline self-talk.* All of us talk to ourselves. This morning in the car I talked to myself about this chapter. If I hadn't had this concern, I might have thought about investments, golf, or half a dozen other things.

During an emergency, I can't afford that. I have to discipline the details—even my self-talk—to pick up time.

The basic difference between fast golfers and slow golfers is planning. The fast golfer thinks about what he's going to do with the ball before he gets to it. He can step up and hit it in a hurry. The slow golfer doesn't think ahead about the shot.

Going to a meeting, I say to myself, *What do I want to come out of the meeting with?* It's clear in my mind if I have talked it over with myself. I walk into the meeting with my agenda set and don't waste time.

18. *Put curiosity on hold.* When I am strapped for time, I have to swallow my curiosity and not ask questions. I make statements. Normally in good human relations, we ask questions. But if we want to save time, we don't.

If we ask, "How's your mother-in-law?" it often takes some time to hear the whole sad story. It's just as warm to say, "Hey, I'm glad to see you," and keep going. Curiosity costs a lot of time.

Let's say I see a group in the hallway, and I wonder what's going on there. If I enter the conversation, I'll stay and talk—and there goes my time.

19. *Stay out of sight.* During a period of emergency I work at home, lay low. The last thing I would do as a pastor is wander

through the church, because somebody will surely stop me and want to talk. Some pastors think that wherever two or three are gathered together, there they should be—knowing what's going on.

I try to curb my exposure during a time of emergency. If I stay out of people's sight, I don't have to offend them with my hurry.

20. *Leave meetings first.* I've had some fun with executives on this point. I tell them the most important person in the meeting leaves it first. Once I finish my speech, that remark empties the hall faster than anything I've ever used before.

Actually, it's true: the most productive people leave a meeting first. They don't stand around shaking hands and swapping stories. A friend of mine sat on a corporate board with me. At the conclusion of one meeting after he had retired, he leaned back in his chair and told a joke. It was the first time in forty-three years! I thought to myself, *He has definitely retired.*

People hang around a meeting to be liked, not to accomplish anything. The business is done; only the social frills are left. A pastor may not be like a salesman who pours drinks until the wee hours of the night to make a sale, but he may hang around a meeting being the nice guy, talking to everybody, trying to get to know everybody, and using too much time for too little profit. Busy people using a time battle plan can't afford the leisure.

That's the checklist for waging the battle.

Don't get me wrong. This plan is not at all about how to speed up. Pastors are already going fast enough. What I'm getting at is how to *gain* some time. I don't care if you loaf in your new-found time. In fact, you ought to use part of it for loafing. If you're already panicky, harried, frantic, and worn out from the pressure, don't spend your new time doing more work, or you'll be right back in the same problem.

I asked a friend one time, "What's a living wage for you?"

He replied, "A little bit more than I'm making now." If I gave him that much more, three months later he'd probably say the same thing again, because he would raise his standard of living to whatever he earns.

If you treat your time like that, you will never be out from under the pressure. If every time you get an hour, you fill it up, you'll have no concept of what a normal lifestyle is.

Our responsibility, our talent, and our time are all given by God. If he can't balance these, who can? One of the most unstressing things I ever discovered was that God could exist after I died! That was most revealing. Why should I feel all this pressure? After all, what would change between the moment I'm doing all this work and the moment I'm dead? Nothing as far as God is concerned. So I don't have to fret; he didn't intend me to live with all this pressure.

A man I know, a very successful professional, paid fifty thousand dollars—money on the table—to go to an alcoholism clinic. One of the most discerning things I've ever heard came from a psychiatrist there. He said.

"For a long time people couldn't understand how a man could be an alcoholic, sober up, stay sober for ten years, and then go back to drinking. Surely he knew all the problems he had as a drunk. Why go back?

"They found out why. People who give up alcohol but remain only *abstainers* can be back to drinking at any time. Those who move from abstaining to *the joy of sobriety* seldom return. But until they make that transition from abstaining to sobriety, they are vulnerable."

There is a theological truth here. If all I have in life is work and more work, without assurance of God's sovereignty, I may well give up the Christian warfare. But if ever I taste the joy of grace, as Paul did, I will see life as a challenge, not a threat. No one could ever sell Paul again on works. He had come out of law to the joy of grace.

In respect to time, we need to move beyond fighting battles, losing them, fighting again, losing again, and fighting once more. We must move to a new way of life. Waging a battle is certainly better than not winning at all. But battles remain second-best to achieving a lifestyle where we stop worrying about time control. It has become so ingrained, so natural and effective—even so joyful—that we wouldn't give it up for anything.

I've provided a battle plan. It will work in a pinch. How much better to win the war.

SIX

WINNING THE WAR FOR TIME

Leaders are not impetuous. They keep a balance between emotional drive and sound thinking. Enthusiasm stimulates their energy.

A short battle for time can be won with the techniques of the previous chapter. But you can only win the *war* with a philosophical base. You have to face such questions as *"Why* do I want to get more out of time? Is it my fear of God or judgment? Is it because I want to become famous or make money? Am I part of a peer group that always seems busy? What's the real reason to squeeze more into my days and weeks?"

These days, haste has become almost a status symbol. People assume, *If I'm busier than you are, I must be more important.* They don't wait for planes to stop before they're up grabbing coats and carry-on luggage. They drive their cars aggressively, trying to get someplace thirty seconds sooner.

I was in a cafeteria recently, and a fellow was trying to get past me to the cashier. I could tell I was supposed to be impressed with the fact he was so busy.

Maybe I've missed something, but I always thought if you were successful, you had *more* time, not less. That's why they used to call the wealthy "the leisure class." In fact, the ancient Greeks made a great case for succeeding in life, reasoning that only those with leisure could think about ideas, which was, after all the highest calling, the mark of true achievement. But these days, as Donald Bloesch puts it, "busyness is the new holiness." Lack of time is a status symbol, and that, to me, is backwards. If you really are somebody, you are in control of your time.

What, then, ought to be our approach to time? Do we assume that time is meant to be used to the fullest (a very American idea)? We need to know what we're after if we're going to win the war for time.

Personally, I think optimizing opportunities and talents—in a sense, bringing redemption to everything around—is a valid reason to use time well. This arises from my philosophical cornerstones:

1. I'm a created being and therefore responsible to the Creator for my life.

2. Time is simply life's clock. Time is a tool—a means in life, never an end. (The same is true of money, by the way; that's why we used to speak about "men of means." Now we call them rich people, which shows how our thinking has moved, and money has become an end in itself.) Time is not something to be pursued for its own sake but for what can be done with it.

3. Since my life is measured by time, I have a responsibility to control it. Most of us don't let other people spend our money; likewise, we should limit their power to spend our time, also.

4. I have been given the same amount of time each day as everybody else. The great achievers of the world don't have any more time than I do. It is simply untrue to say, "I don't have enough time." What is *not* the same for everybody is energy. Unless I recognize my level of energy and realize that it comes in ebbs and surges, I won't accomplish all I could.

5. I also believe that anything I cannot accomplish in the time I have is apparently not my God-given responsibility to accomplish. God is not going to hold me accountable for what I cannot do because of genuine lack of time.

6. When I know the ultimate purpose of my life, I can know

whether I'm using my time properly. If I do not know that ultimate purpose, I have no way of judging my efficiency. Only God and I can know for sure whether I'm wasting time or using it wisely.

Charles Francis Adams, the nineteenth-century political figure and diplomat, kept a diary. One day he entered: "Went fishing with my son today—a day wasted." His son, Brook Adams, also kept a diary, which is still in existence. On that same day Brook Adams made this entry: "Went fishing with my father—the most wonderful day of my life!"

I decided a long time ago that my ultimate goal in life was to stretch other people. I wanted them to live a bit better, fuller, bigger, more nobly than if they hadn't met me. This is my sense of redeeming human situations.

When I was a young man, I would jot items to talk about on a little card in my shirt pocket. Instead of making small talk (and knowing that most people don't care what they talk about), I thought it would be profitable to talk about subjects on which I wanted to expand my thinking. I found I had certain viewpoints I wanted to sell. I would work up little outlines to get them across. I would maneuver the situation around to practice my "teaching."

As I have gotten older, my agenda has been trying to determine what help the other person needs that I can give. I try to discover the person's immediate problems. Maybe something in my experience can be helpful. I can take a little extra time and say, "What do you see in life? What's interesting? What kind of problems are you facing?" without prying or being curious. This has moved me from teaching a subject to counseling a need.

With a goal in life and an intent in each conversation, I think I'm more efficient, more effective.

Spending Time or Investing It?

There are two ways to approach time. One is the technological: minutes as units. The other is the philosophical: minutes as meaning. It's possible to grasp the technological view so tightly that you end up with no meaning. Technology should always be the servant of philosophy.

Too often people don't know the difference between a fast track and a frantic track. I enjoy a fast-track life, but I don't relish being frantic. It's just as foolish to use every minute for activity as it is to spend every nickel you've got. I know some high-income folk who think they've got to spend all their money.

A young man in commercial real estate once asked me, "Would you help me with a financial problem?"

"What is it?"

"Well, I earn big commissions—but they're spaced out."

"I've had some experience with that," I said. "I'll be happy to show you how to budget under those conditions."

I began talking, but pretty soon he interrupted. "Mr. Smith, you don't understand. In between the commissions, my wife and I get behind on our spending. And by the time we catch up on our spending, we don't have enough money to pay our bills."

I went dumb. I had no way to understand that mentality.

Later on, I realized it explained why a lot of people will never be financially responsible. They have an innate feeling of *having to spend!* They're supposed to live like the neighbors, and by the time they catch up on their spending *responsibility*—they are not able to pay the bills. They live frantically.

In the same way, some people think they *have* to spend time, use it up one way or another—while others invest it. My philosophy is to invest, which means looking for a return on what I do. Some of that return will be in dollars or other visible achievement, but some will be more internal. Investing time wisely does something for you. Over a period of time it brings an appreciation, a patina to life; it generates maturity and fullness.

Not long ago, while waiting to speak to a group, there was a flowery introduction, and I filled the time by calculating in my mind how many days I had lived. I came to something over twenty-five thousand, and I thought, *My goodness—a fellow* OUGHT *to be able to accomplish something in that amount of time. He ought to be able to do almost anything.*

When you're investing time instead of spending it, you don't get so concerned about running out. That's what a midlife crisis is: thinking about all the time already gone, the things you haven't done, won't get to do—and you get frantic. By contrast, people who invest their time (many rural people, for example) move through the middle years in a much more mature way.

The technological view of time is not wrong. It includes scheduling, digital thinking, techniques, telephone efficiency, learning to do two things at once—anybody with a fairly bright mind can learn them. But the philosophical goes beyond the mind to matters of the spirit.

Many people don't know how to invest their time because they have never identified their unique purpose in life. They have instead settled for comfort. They've climbed the organization chart until they found a comfortable income or responsibility—and they've pitched their tent permanently.

Americans are known for seeking comfort and convenience. What this amounts to is settling for life as a consumer rather than a producer. A philosophical approach to life says, "I am a producer, not just a consumer; I must leave behind something extra, some worthwhile evidence that I passed by this way."

How Much Is Enough?

Most pastors are, of course, committed to a lifestyle of giving. Yet they still struggle in the war for time. Why?

Anyone who tries to meet the needs of people soon finds there is no end of demand for services. What can make this situation livable? I believe the solution lies in stating that your purpose in life is to accomplish what is uniquely *you*, not just whatever comes along.

There will never be a lack of needs. We can go absolutely

berserk trying to meet everyone's needs. But they are not ours to meet. We're playing God when we get into that kind of compulsion.

Opportunity is not a mandate to *do*. Your mandate comes from what you have *chosen* to try to accomplish.

If my ultimate goal is to stretch people, then I have to decide where I can be most effective. If a farmer has a bushel of corn and several different fields in which to plant it, he will pick the most fertile field. In the same way, I will spend lots of time with someone who has potential for growth instead of spreading it out over ten people who have little potential.

These choices demonstrate the fact that it is more important for a leader to be respected than to be liked. If you are respected, you can influence people. You cannot influence them just by being a good ol' boy. Think about a medical doctor. I don't care how pleasant he is—if most of his patients die, he's not the doctor I'm looking for.

Many times, our "counseling" deteriorates into social chats. The hours tick by, but how many people's attitudes and actions are changed? That is the question.

Earning Respect for Your Time

People respect us when we can get to the problem quickly. There's something professional about that. If through reading as well as living we have developed the intuition, knowledge, and experience to be helpful to others, and if we have the courage to go right at the issue and not be afraid of conflict, people will see we mean business with our time.

Even when I must say, "I think I understand the issue, but I can't help you; that's not the kind of problem I can treat," the person may not like me very much, but he or she will respect me.

I also do not give advice; I give observations and list options. I don't feel I should take responsibility for what other people do. They ought to make the decision. I will say, "Here's the problem, and here are two or three options I see for you. Now, which are you going to choose? Or do you see other options?"

The next time I see that person, I won't say, "Hey, how ya doin'?" I'll say, "How are you getting along on that particular issue? Which option did you choose? How is it working out?"

Once people find out you're going to hold them accountable, the frivolous counseling requests dry up.

I believe in practicing this approach myself, by the way. When I went to the doctor with high blood pressure, he said, "Why don't you try losing a little weight?"

In five weeks, I lost twenty-six pounds, which greatly surprised my doctor. But I told him, "Dick, you're a world-class physician. I haven't got a right to ask you to keep me alive unless I'm willing to match your dedication." I wanted him to know this was a give-give situation.

In the same way, I have no hesitancy about demanding that people respect my time and effort, because I'm convinced after years of doing this that it creates respect. Some will drop out. But we must invest our time, not spend it.

A friend sent an acquaintance to me, the executive vice-president of a large company. He had gotten mad and quit. At age fifty, he was without another job. I saw he had an ego problem and wasn't really trying to find a job. Overrating his reputation, he was sitting around waiting for somebody to call him.

I suggested this to him. Then I called my friend and said, "Your friend may be a little sore, because I put it to him straight."

"That's exactly what you should have said, because it's true," he replied. "But I didn't want to say it because he might not like me."

So *that* was why he sent him to me!

I saw the man later. He had found another job, and even though he didn't particularly enjoy what I did, there was no question that he respected my honesty.

Sympathy and comfort are two very different things. I don't mind spending time comforting someone, but I won't spend time sympathizing. Sympathy is an addictive emotion; people want more and more and more. Comfort, on the other hand, brings a light to the darkness. Comfort produces progress; sympathy doesn't.

This tough approach may not be popular. But I've found it brings respect. Lee Iacocca has succeeded at Chrysler not because people like him, but because they respect him. He produced results.

Even intimate relationships in the church can produce results. Unless people are maturing, their affection for the pastor can sometimes be an inoculation. "I like the preacher and the preacher likes me." What does that mean? Very little. We can get the same closeness at the Rotary Club.

But if you care about people enough to put your life on the line to make them mature, functioning Christians, I suspect fewer and fewer of them will try to waste your time. People who are *doing things* respect not only their own time but others' as well. Strong people have an agenda of their own.

People take a pastor's time seriously if the pastor himself or herself takes it seriously. This is conveyed in small but important ways. For example, you can say, "I hope I won't lose my salvation for this, but the other day I wasted a few minutes, and you folks know what a nut I am about not wasting time." They'll get the message.

You can set definite times for meetings. Even if the calendar is open, you don't say, "Well, come any time Tuesday." Instead, you say, "I'll be glad to see you. How long do you think you'll need?" Or "How long will it take us to accomplish what you've got in mind?" This trains people to think in terms of schedule.

In the same way, you can telegraph your view of time by cutting the conversation off promptly at the end. "Is there anything else profitable that we should talk about, or are we finished?" This establishes the reason we're talking: to accomplish something.

Personal Habits

Not all time losses can be blamed on other people. Some things are entirely within us.

Periodically, we have to review our personal habits—those patterns of behavior we establish to save time and then forget about. Sometimes habits deteriorate without our realizing it, until they are hurtful instead of helpful.

When I was younger, reading was a more valuable exercise than it is now. Why? Back then, I found a new idea on every page, it seemed. Now, having stored away a great deal of material, I'm lucky to get two new ideas per book. So I have to say, "Is my habit of reading as productive as it used to be?"

That doesn't mean I've quit reading. I've simply changed the kinds of things I read. At this point, I do theme reading (if I'm working on a particular project) or else what I call philosophical reading. I want to stay close to certain writers, even though I already know what they have to say. I read Oswald Chambers, for example, nearly every day. I want to maintain a personal relationship with his type of thinking, his personality.

Sometimes people read for ego reasons. They shop the best-seller list. Someone says, "Have you read so-and-so?" and they hate to admit they haven't, so they go buy the book or at least catch a review. This takes a tremendous amount of time. That is one reason the reading habit has to be reviewed every so often to be sure it's still productive.

Another area to consider is driving time. It's gotten very popular to listen to tapes in the car. I do a lot of this myself. But I heard a bright man say he hates tapes because he can read so much faster than anyone can talk. Why take the time to listen when he can get the material in half or even one third the time in written form?

Another problem of tape listening in the car is that you can't make notes while you listen. You're really only screening to see whether anything on the tape is worth listening to.

Many times in an automobile, we ought to be quiet. Who

says listening to tapes is better than being quiet? My wife and I sometimes drive a hundred miles and don't say a word. She may be reading, while I'm thinking about some subject, and both of us are making profitable use of the time.

What about the habit of the "business lunch"? In my judgment, eating together is generally only a preface to conversation. You eat for forty-five minutes before you ever get down to business. It might establish rapport, but it's hard to do serious business. I would rather have thirty minutes eyeballing somebody in an office than two hours over a dinner table. Eating is a social occasion, not the most productive business occasion.

In my city, it's almost a fad for professional people to have breakfast together. I mean, if you eat breakfast at home, something must be wrong with you. You're not one of the movers. Such fads have to be reviewed. We have to ask, "Am I really accomplishing anything?"

Now, I do some breakfasts, usually at seven o'clock. I use this technique to find out who's really serious about meeting with me. I've even been known to say to someone who wanted counseling, "Fine—I'll meet you at six o'clock for breakfast." It is amazing how many back off.

But I remember one man who took me up on it and was waiting at the table armed with a big legal pad and a tape recorder. I probably helped him as much as anybody I ever tried to help. We've maintained a relationship all through the years because he was serious.

On the other hand, if a person wants to see me but admits he doesn't really have anything definite in mind, I'll propose lunch. After all, I have to eat anyway. Lunch is a good block of time to at least develop a relationship.

Organized Versus Orderly

In all of this, it's important to know the difference between orderliness and organization. People who are too fastidious turn orderliness into an end rather than a means—and that takes a lot of time. It's much more important to be organized.

If you watch A students study, they just study. C students, on the other hand, get ready to study. They get a Coke. They get the pencil sharpened. They lay everything out in a certain format. What they're doing is avoiding studying by preparing.

A certain amount of orderliness is necessary, of course, but as long as I know how to do my job effectively, I'm organized—and no amount of orderliness will help. A lot of people are orderly because they want to appear organized. When guests come to our house, my wife is always saying, "Be sure to keep your study door closed; I'd hate for them to think that's the way we live." But I'd let anybody go in there who's a *worker*, and they'd see exactly why things are like they are.

We have to guard against perfectionism. Very few things in this world are worth perfecting, and it takes a tremendous amount of time to perfect anything. If you're going to move your golf game from seventy-five to seventy-two, you're going to have to practice a lot more than if you're moving from ninety to eighty-five. Every point down the scale requires an increase in time and effort.

If you're perfecting something because you feel, under God, that it needs perfecting, that's one thing. But if you're doing it so people will say how good you are . . . or because you're afraid of criticism, that's wasteful. You must decide the degree of perfection your work requires.

I've known speakers who were no more effective without notes than they were with notes. But because they wanted to be complimented, they spent unwarranted amounts of time getting ready to speak without notes.

Actually, the things you can do best, you can do fastest. Most people do not really appreciate what they can do best because it's too much fun! They have a puritanical concept of work that says it's supposed to be difficult. This makes a person's specialty feel like leisure or entertainment, not "work"—and that becomes a trap. Fast isn't always bad.

Temptations

Sometimes we can outwit ourselves in the war for time. I've noticed three temptations that pull us aside.

1 — The first is procrastination. If I ever get around to it, I'm going to run for president of the National Procrastination Society. I just haven't quite gotten around to it.

An executive startled me once by saying he wasn't taking his briefcase home anymore. I asked why, and he said, "Well, I analyzed my work, and all day long I was sorting papers to take home at night. I found out I might as well just go ahead and make decisions and stop sorting papers."

A lot of procrastination is based on our fear of action. We review and review and review. I spoke for a preacher not long ago who said he hated Sundays because he hates to preach. What he really hates is to prepare his sermon. He wouldn't mind preaching at all if he would go ahead and commit the time to his sermon, but he won't do it. This in turn produces guilt, which drains intensity. Time means nothing if you don't have energy to focus.

2 — The second temptation is rationalization: trying to prove to yourself you weren't wrong. It would be so much easier to say, "I messed up. It wasn't the audience's fault; I simply wasn't 'on' tonight." That would save a lot of time.

3 — The third is indecision. I once knew an executive who had a sign on his desk: THE DEFINITE ANSWER IS MAYBE. And he worked unbelievable hours. Instead of deciding, he would mull around and talk to people about the decision and delay and. . . .

Maxey Jarman once said to me, "Many people can make good decisions, but they *won't*." Because that means putting their ego on the line.

I see this in a lot of seminary students. They delay making decisions until there is no other decision to make. Then they glorify it by saying it was God's will. For example, they come to school to "find God's will for my life," stay three or four years, spend all their money, go into debt, get married, and have kids. By the time graduation comes, what alternative is there besides going into the ministry? By their indecision they've been forced into a certain track for reasons that have more to do with economics than God's will.

Besides these three temptations, we have to curb certain ― ⁴⁄ self-destructive tendencies.

We have to try to stay healthy. If a person is sick twenty days a year, that's an obvious time loss; most people don't need to be sick more than a couple of days a year. Most overweight people run short of energy, and when you don't have enough energy, you can't make good use of time.

Financial problems are another enemy of concentration. There's a holiness in paying your bills. As I told a group of singles recently, "When the preacher says on Sunday, 'Go in peace,' you can't obey if your budget is in pieces and you're facing the bill collector Monday." That's true of leaders as well. I've seen people spend inordinate amounts of time fussing with bills, because they simply couldn't delay gratification. M. Scott Peck, the psychiatrist, says the greatest sin in America is this inability to delay gratification.

These temptations are like magnetic fields that must be kept away from computer software. If we are not careful, they will erase our ability to perform.

Time Out

The last part of the war plan for time is the necessity of time out. I guard two things in life: savings and time alone. I simply must have two days every so often to talk to nobody. Otherwise, I can't stay in control of myself. I can't feel I am directing my life.

This, again, is why I look forward to time in an automobile. Too many people ride along looking at everybody, listening to the radio or a tape, complaining about the other drivers and the heavy traffic. They never stop to think of a car as a wonderful cocoon, a monastery, a holy cave.

Time with just a few special people is also strategic. Somebody called me the other day and asked me to speak at a Christian convention. I said, "I can't do it, because Mary Alice and I are going out to Colorado and play golf."

There was this strange silence on the other end.

So I said, "It's important. There are four couples going out, and the other three wouldn't have anybody to beat if I didn't go. It's part of my ministry."

I was being a little facetious—but not much. People lose sight of the fact that relaxation is part of the foundation of one's contribution. How can you do any thinking if you don't spend time alone, unpressured, refreshed?

Sometimes I feel like I'm a kid with a quarter in a candy store trying to decide what to buy. Time is my quarter, and once I've swapped it for jelly beans or chocolate stars, I don't want to be unhappy. So I have to choose with care.

In order to make wise choices, I must know my philosophy of what's good and what's not—and even with that, I will need to ask for help sometimes. Some of the busiest people I know don't really need to be so busy. They just can't bring themselves to ask for help.

I ask people because I think they really can help; I've seen something in their life or their track record that proves they have some experience to share. An awful lot of people know an awful lot more than I do about an awful lot of things. I envision myself as a football coach, and they are my "bench." If I need extra strength, I go to the bench for somebody to help me out. I say to these people, "What are you reading that's good? What have you read that I don't have to read? Tell me the major points." They like to do it, and I get the benefit.

In these ways I maximize the opportunities not just to save time but to use it profitably.

S E V E N

SELECTING YOUR INNER CIRCLE

The leader will take counsel from his people, but he will act on what his mind tells him is right. He has trained himself out of the fear of making mistakes.

T he secret of any organization's success is choosing the right people to play key roles.

I read recently about business executive Bernard Tapie, who became famous in France by taking over failing corporations (often for one symbolic franc) and turning them into successful money makers. Tapie developed an empire of forty-five companies, including Look ski bindings and Terraillon, a weight scale manufacturer. His secret? Whenever he assumed control of a corporation, he immediately brought in his fifteen-member management team to reorganize. They worked so well together that they salvaged many a corporation.

One of the most important aspects of successful leadership is putting together a group of people to carry out the mission. Great athletic coaches know they must have talent to win, and therefore they take an active part in choosing players. Teams that just happen get happenstance results.

Much of this chapter will deal specifically with building a church staff. I recognize that many pastors will never be in a position to hire professional associates. But every pastor will, like Jesus, gather a group of committed followers—disciples—who will carry out the vision. These key individuals may be paid staff or committed volunteers, but they are the ones who see that ministry happens. Thus, the pastor's "inner circle" is perhaps the most important part of the organization. It is this group I mean when I henceforth refer to "staff."

Staffing is a vexation in the church, partly because it is innately difficult and partly because church leaders get so little practice. But it remains extremely important. Small organizations such as churches often make the mistake of thinking they can get by with inferior workers because they are small. The opposite is true. In a firm of one hundred employees, if one is inferior, the loss is only 1 percent. But if a church has a staff of three, and one is inferior, the loss is 33 percent.

The bright side, however, is that it's much easier to pick one excellent person than a hundred.

Attracting quality people, first of all, means you must enthusiastically sell your organization to quality people. Julian Price, the builder of Jefferson Standard Life Insurance Company, surprised many by his ability to get outstanding people to join his organization when it was still tiny. He did it with his optimism, telling prospective workers, "We're going to build a mighty company here; don't you want to be a part of it?" The challenge of growth has brought many great talents to small organizations.

Church leaders needn't be timid in going for the most effective people. We believe what we're doing is the most important of all endeavors.

Perhaps the more difficult part of recruiting is recognizing the quality people. Here are seven qualities I look for.

Qualities for the Core

The first thing I want is *character*. I used to put intelligence first, but I changed my mind. I found I could buttress a person's intelligence, but I could not buttress character.

A job applicant with a weak character will do a lot to hide it, of course. Many people have told me they had a lot to learn about the job I was trying to fill, but no one ever admitted to having a weak character and needing help.

Statistically, however, most management failures come from lack of character rather than lack of intelligence. You can do many things to help a person intellectually, but you are completely vulnerable to the person with a weak character. The weakness will show up at the moment of highest stress, at the very time you need the person to stand.

I have found that adults seldom correct their character faults. Personalities may change, but character rarely does. After doing something wrong, they may be sincerely sorry, but then they trip again over the same stumbling block. If I know the person's weakness, I may be able to structure around it, but often it's too late when I find it.

As Christians, we want to help the weak, but the church staff—the inner circle—is no halfway house for character problems. I warn new managers against trying to do social reclamation in administration.

Character is not homogeneous, like a quart of milk. It is sectional, like a grapefruit. Everyone has good sections and bad. One person may be strongly loyal to the boss, for example, but irresponsible in the job. Another person may be loyal and responsible until he gets a chance to enhance his ego. Ego will weaken character as much as anything I know. Willie Sutton, the bank robber, loved his work but cried when he had to lie to his mother about where he had been. You can't say he had a totally bad character; you can only say some sections were bad.

As a manager you must evaluate all the sections, build on the good ones, and avoid the weak ones. If you have trouble evaluating character, get someone with good insight to help you.

Second, a person must have enough *intelligence* to do the job and also be a possibility for promotion. I am never afraid of gathering too much intelligence in any organization.

This is particularly true in the church, which has no real limit on its possibilities for growth. A business might have capital or territorial limits, but there are few limits on a church that the right staff cannot break through. So pastors should insist on above-average job competence.

3— Third, I want a person who is *flexible*—and who doesn't confuse flexibility with lack of integrity. Some people accuse others at times of lacking integrity, when the issue has nothing to do with that. The only thing at stake is flexibility.

One of the things that indicates a healthy flexibility is optimism. Positive people look upon change as challenge, and they go for it without hesitation.

Some people have a magnetism for iron; no matter who they deal with, they are always attracted to whatever good is in the person. Others have an allergy for clay; they break out in hives over whatever is bad in the people they meet.

Church members, of course, sometimes have a great deal of clay, and people who have the allergy can't even sit next to them in church. They keep wondering why the pastor doesn't preach against the clay. The pastor, meanwhile, has a magnetism for iron; he is constantly finding the good in people and encouraging it. The clay hardly bothers him.

Churches need to be staffed with flexible people who go for the iron and aren't bothered by the clay.

Those with an allergy to clay are perhaps better off in an evangelistic organization, where they can proclaim their faith to large numbers of people they see only once. But those who have to work with the same people fifty-two weeks a year had better be magnetized to iron.

As far as integrity is concerned, I am more anxious that a person be consistent than that he or she always be minutely right. Sometimes a baseball broadcaster will say, "The pitcher's establishing the strike zone," meaning he's throwing the ball high, low, in, and out, trying to find out what this particular umpire considers the zone to be. What's important is how he's going to rule throughout the game. Once I establish what a staff member will consistently do, I know how to work with the person and in what areas I can trust him.

4 — Fourth, I like to have people around me who are *excited about learning*. Their rates of learning change over time, of

course, but if they are not oriented to growth, if they prefer instead to protect the status quo, I will have a stagnant organization.

Nothing helps a staff grow more than a leader who wants to grow. I like to watch Leonard Bernstein conduct a symphony. He lets the musicians see what great music does to him. He inspires them while he conducts, and that's what every executive should do. The orchestra enjoys pleasing Bernstein.

Fifth, as soon as the number of staff members begins to increase, I must pick *team players*. A true team player does not poach on other people's responsibility but is available to help at their request. When he sits in a meeting, he is open in his remarks; he does not go around making comments privately, either suggestions or criticisms. He speaks up in the meeting.

A team player, however, is not the same as a yes man. Some managers have a hard time knowing the difference. A yes man gets along with the boss, but the other team members ostracize him. And whenever the boss points him out as exemplary, the rest get sick at their stomachs. They lose respect for both the boss and the yes man.

Sixth, the inner circle must be willing and able to *confront in a healthy manner*. This means the leader must be willing to listen to those who differ.

I was with a pastor recently who had built a five-thousand-member church, but he was resigning to go into politics. His followers said God was moving him on; they had no criticism of him at all. And yet he's leaving the church $4.5 million in debt, which it may never be able to pay off. His charisma is tremendous, but his management is not. And apparently there was no one on the inner circle who was able to say early enough, "Hey, we're creating a debt structure we can't handle."

One of the church members told me, "Nobody is able to stop him from doing anything he wants. He's so strong." Well, for his own protection he should have somebody to prevent those kinds of mistakes.

When I was with Genesco, we had several individuals I called "corporate cockleburs." Their function was to irritate us. One by the name of Lou got me so angry in a board meeting that afterward I said to Maxey Jarman, our president, "You can't pay me enough to sit in a meeting with that guy."

Maxey said, "Does he irritate you? Then he's earning his salary, because his greatest function is to irritate." I recognized later that Lou was also basically right in what he had said. He regularly took the devil's-advocate position to test our proposals. He kept us from making mistakes.

If your inner circle is always in agreement, you run the risk of blind spots and letting your mistakes get outside your control. This is what happened in the Nixon White House. No one inside the circle blew the whistle on Watergate, so the whole administration tumbled. The ability to confront with integrity and correct with care is a valuable quality.

Finally, I want a person who is *comfortable being reviewed*. In business, of course, we do this regularly; we even have departments that specialize in reviewing procedure. Job descriptions tell us what the person should have been doing, and periodically we assess the performance.

But in a Christian setting, many workers seem to resist review. They feel they have been called by God, and therefore the pastor, board, or department head is not really their supervisor—God is. If their concept of what God wants them to do (which is usually what they happen to enjoy doing) conflicts with what the organization expects of them, it's too bad for the organization.

Such an attitude brings havoc into the work of the kingdom. Extended prayer time in the morning is no excuse for showing up late for work. Good managers have to make these things clear. I want persons in my organization who are subject to review, who receive it willingly, and who profit from it.

Seeking and Finding

How can we find and recruit such people? One of the first things to realize is that we are not hiring friends. We are gathering assistants and associates—capable people who are able to do what we cannot do, perhaps able to do things better than we ever could.

I do not have to be chummy with the person, and he or she does not have to like me. But we must respect each other. A lot of leaders make the mistake of hiring people they like rather than people they respect. They end up choosing individuals just like themselves, duplicating their own strengths and weaknesses, which does not advance the overall organization.

Hiring is often a disagreeable chore because it comes at a bad time. We are disappointed that someone has just left, we're short-handed and anxious to fill a vacancy before the roof falls in. So we do not select carefully; we rush things.

Actually, the higher the position to be filled, the more time we should spend filling it. We have a responsibility to the persons we choose, because if they don't work out, we will have to replace them.

Quick interviews simply do not tell enough. What often happens is that the interviewer is something of a salesman and, instead of making the person prove his ability, he wastes time selling the job. If the person leaves having not accepted, the interviewer feels as if he failed.

The opposite should be happening: The hiring person should be the customer, not the salesman. I refuse to hire a person who does not say something along the way that makes me hire him. I assume this person will not make it until I am convinced otherwise. When it comes to hiring, I am not trying to be benevolent; I am on a search for outstanding qualities.

And the search takes time. The right person may not convince me in the first twenty minutes. That is why, if I am hiring a man, I like to travel with him. You can find out so much on a three-day trip. You gain insight into the person's physical energy. You find out whether he has a large intellectual cup or a small one. A person with a small intellectual cup is quickly satisfied; he listens to a ten-minute sermon or presentation, and he's set for the week. No curious questions, no asking for proof of your statements, no ongoing dialogue; his cup is already full.

Such a person may be exactly the one you want—for certain jobs. Some work is very monotonous, and you do not want people with too much curiosity in such a position. But for other jobs, you need an individual with large intellectual thirst.

As I travel, I watch the person read a newspaper. I notice what sections he turns to quickly and what stories he reads. I also watch how he dresses for various occasions. One of the finest Christians I know is entirely too casual about his dress. He does not realize how this creates disrespect for his leadership. He feels it shouldn't, and perhaps he is right—but it does. This is one of the tests of leadership: that you recognize what affects people, not what *should* affect people.

On the road, I also notice how courteous a person is. I watch how he treats doormen, taxi drivers, waitresses. How he tips is a big indicator for me. I see how careful the person is about being on time. I simply cannot work with someone who does not respect a schedule. Some are not offended by this, but I am.

Perhaps I learn the most by riding with the person, letting him or her drive. An automobile magnifies the average person's sense of power. I find out how this person watches the pattern of events. If he drives in a constant state of emergency, slamming on his brakes, speeding up to get out of somebody's way, or wandering from lane to lane, I make a mental note that this person is not a good planner. He doesn't look ahead and watch the patterns form in advance.

If he berates other drivers for creating a problem, or if he constantly harps against the city for how it maintains the streets, this tells me something else. It tells me this person has a hard time accepting problems and circumstances beyond his control. Successful people work within the limits of what they can control and don't waste their energy on other things.

In the car, I also notice the person's respect for property. The way he or she treats an automobile tells me how he will treat my company's typewriters, computers, and other equipment in the future. I'm amazed at the people who will run right over a chuckhole; either they are not watching the road-way, or they don't want to make the effort to avoid the hole. Again, this is not a good managerial mentality.

Do you think I am too exacting? I simply want to know what to watch out for. My philosophy is to utilize a person's strengths and buttress his weaknesses. But until I know the weaknesses, I cannot do anything to buttress them.

Personnel evaluation is not the time for extending Christian tolerance. The whole idea of evaluation is to be objective. Hence, prejudice is out—but so is tolerance. The art of good management is to avoid being surprised. If I do not evaluate people to the best of my ability, I will face constant surprises.

The reason why references are so useless in Christian circles is that they are usually sabotaged by tolerance. No one wants to blow the whistle. I think it is my Christian responsibility to be as objective as I can when giving a reference. This has gotten me into trouble; I've been on several boards where I ended up being the bearer of bad news, simply because the rest of the members knew I would do it. They all rationalized that I must enjoy this kind of thing, and they saved their popularity in the process.

A law firm once told me they paid almost no attention to references anymore; they could learn everything they wanted to know by studying the person's history instead. Their belief was that successful people will be successful in the future, and failures will be failures. They also found that most failures are very adept at explaining their failures, and when you start buying failure stories, you are only presenting an opportunity to fail again.

There is a lot of wisdom here. I believe in going all the way back to check school records, because winners start winning very early. They form good habits, they show a sense of responsibility, they respond well to authority, they are able to organize themselves.

A Harvard study of business people showed that, actually, there are very few late bloomers. The things that make for professional success are usually apparent in student days.

I also believe in running a credit check. I'm very interested in whether a person pays bills promptly or not.

Furthermore, I have learned I cannot ferret out everything about the person myself. That is why I arrange multiple interviews, using other people who have good intuition. Some people have a knack for asking very clear questions that seem to plumb the depths of a person.

For example, my wife is one of the finest judges of character I've ever known. When she says she likes somebody, I have learned to expect good character—a person who is trustworthy, friendly, kind, and has integrity. She's almost infallible.

I never question her evaluations, and I never make her defend them. That's one of the worst things you can do to intuitive people. They can no more prove their intuitions than they can prove their faith. But they will still be right most of the time.

I also want the immediate supervisor and colleagues to interview the prospect. Some dictators will disagree with me here, because they don't want to give the impression the hiring is being done by a group. But if a person is going to work with certain people, they should help make the decision—and it is good to get them on record recommending the newcomer. They will accept him or her with a great deal more grace; they will help him along and create a good environment, because they have a stake in his success.

When a new person starts having problems, I have been known to challenge those who helped me interview as to why—and then watch them work very hard to get him out of his problems!

When someone came to apply for a machine job in my plant, I often asked, "Who do you know in this plant?" He would name two or three people on the shop floor, and then I'd go see them.

"Your friend came in and wanted a job," I'd say. "If you were me, would you hire him?"

If something was wrong, the employee would invariably

say, "Well, let's not overdo that 'friend' business: I know him, but he's not really what you'd call a friend." He didn't want me coming around a month later saying, "Look, you recommended this guy, and he's no good."

We must always be careful, and we must not be arrogant about our own ability to choose people. Most of us can be conned. Most of us tend to want to sell the job and make everyone happy. We must force ourselves to be deliberate and objective.

When You Make a Hiring Mistake

No one wants a reputation as a hatchet man. But as a last resort, you must be willing to fire people or relieve them of a particular responsibility. It is more important for the staff to know that you will than that you do. It shows you are committed to your mission and are willing to prune those who will not contribute to it.

How should a person be dismissed? It depends on the reason for dismissal:

1. *Character problems.* In such a case, there is no reason to delay. You may not always need to make the person a public example, but you should move swiftly.

2. *Personality conflicts.* First of all, consider whether this person might work out in a different spot in the organization. I have moved troublemakers who happened to be very capable people, because it seemed they would have been fine working alone. So I have talked to them straight, told them exactly what was wrong, and given them another chance in a new assignment.

Some have straightened up; more have not. I had to keep watching the problem and not consider it solved, of course, as time went on. And in many cases, the only final solution was to let them go.

3. *Irresponsibility, shoddy work.* A manager begins by documenting, gathering enough specific information about errors or bad judgments to support the charge. If I am convinced a

person has gotten into a mental state of "I'm going to do as little as I can get by with," then I try to inject a good, hot spark of fear. There is something in all of us that profits from that occasionally. I need to get scared every once in a while myself. It helps my humility, it boosts my effort, and it focuses my concentration tremendously.

Whenever I am tempted not to act in a difficult personnel situation, I ask myself, "Am I holding back for my personal comfort or for the good of the organization?" If I am doing what makes me comfortable, I am embezzling. If doing what is good for the organization also happens to make me comfortable, that's wonderful. But if I am treating irresponsibility irresponsibly, I must remember that two wrongs do not make a right.

When Not to Fire

If, however, a staff member is failing because of inadequate training, that is a different story. We must be patient and provide training; that is part of our Christian duty as leaders.

The long view will serve us well in all matters of hiring and staffing. Part of leadership is anticipating problems before they fester. We must sit down occasionally and ask, "What is going to be the result of what we're doing now? How will the relationships among these people look in two years, in five years? Who is growing? Who is not growing? Who is accepting responsibility and doing a good job? Who isn't?" Pastors are wise to have a formal or informal review committee with whom they can sit and assess personnel strengths and weaknesses confidentially. From this they can project together what kind of church they will have down the road.

If they want to grow in a certain ministry, and they see the individual in charge of that area cannot carry it where they want to go, they can deal with that problem in a prudent and thoughtful way. Can the person be trained, or must he be replaced?

The well-run organization is not a place of high drama, with many sudden elevations to power and heart-rending lurches into the street. It is a place where people are carefully chosen and guided to work together to fulfill goals bigger than all of them.

EIGHT

TRAINING THE CORE WORKERS

Leaders must steer a wary course between keeping their fingers in every pie, dictating in detail what is to be done by whom, and on the other hand slackening the rein so that assistants learn only by experience and make costly mistakes.

People have great potential if they want to train themselves. Perhaps the greatest challenge in training someone else is getting the person to want to be trained.

The gateway, I believe, is personal relationship. As I mentioned in the previous chapter, I've never been able to fully motivate a person I didn't like. The same is true of training. I can *instruct* someone I don't like. I can teach a person the expressways of Dallas whether I like him or not, but I could never develop that person's skills and talents.

I learned this from experience. While working with a certain individual, I wasn't making any progress, and I wondered why. Finally I realized I didn't like the man. He was outgoing and had good comprehension skills—but he overrated himself, and that irritated me. I consciously tuned out his bragging, and that prevented me from getting close to him personally.

Finally I realized what was happening, and I began to find other things in him to like. An interesting thing occurred: He began to develop very well.

Before any of us can be trained, we need to believe somebody wants us to do well, believes in us, likes us, respects us.

Train Strengths, Not Weaknesses

In developing somebody, the odds of improving existing strengths far outweigh the odds of improving weaknesses. An individual *can* improve his weaknesses, but it's rarely done from the outside.

You can threaten the person. You can make him afraid. But that won't bring improvement. On the other hand, if you point out strengths and help develop them, you capitalize on the person's desire to do those things he's already good at. (He obviously has no ambition for things he does poorly.)

If a certain weakness is so bad you can't ignore it, you may have to do one of two things: get him to work on it, or admit you can't utilize this person. This amounts to developing someone through fear (the fear of losing his job)—which is far from ideal.

By taking the positive approach, you may awaken a strength the person didn't know he had. I've seen people discover artistic talent in middle life—a craft, painting, music, or something else. Part of training is testing for areas of additional capability.

Training Is Costly

One of the expenses of training is that you commit yourself to people who make mistakes. Mistakes are simply part of the bill, and there's no way to prevent them.

Think about giving a person a new job that has a lot of detail. Until he or she gets familiar with that detail, some things are going to slip. This will cost money and aggravation. But it's part of the training.

When a person first starts to supervise, for example, he often waits too long to handle grievances. They fester. That is why you say, "A grievance has to be handled on time. You can't postpone them. People are the most valuable part of what we do, and they come before our own convenience."

Now, if a person repeatedly makes the same mistake, you have to wonder whether he's in the right position.

If I correct a person, I always want to see the person the next day. If I'm not going to be available the next day, I'll postpone the correction, because people tend to magnify the break in relationship. A correction isn't a relational break at all; you're simply carrying out your responsibility. But that's hard to remember. If I talk to someone at four o'clock about some problem, I try to see him the next morning, speak to him, smile, and show him that what I said was all I was going to say.

Not Everything at Once

Training also has to be paced. People can make only so much progress at a time. Even though you see several things they have to learn, you are wiser to break them into pieces they can handle. Have the patience to give the other pieces as time goes along.

If you assign six things at once, you break the spirit. You break the person's concentration, too; he spends so much time thinking about what's gone wrong or could go wrong that he doesn't do his job. And if there's something about a person he cannot improve—family background, for example, or accent, looks, or spouse—don't even mention it. Development is based on improvability.

In some severe situations, I admit, a spouse's attitude or behavior may actually threaten someone's future. That situation has to be faced—but this is beyond what we call training or development. It's simply a necessary action. You have to say to the person, "If this doesn't change, you're not going to be here. I want you to know why. But it's not my responsibility to change your wife. That is up to you. If at any time you think it would be helpful for me to sit down with you and her and talk it over, I'd be happy to do that. But, since she does not work for me, it's not my responsibility to develop her."

Pacing means not only spreading out our topics but treating

each topic more than once. People rarely get anything the first time you say it. So you vary the wording each time, even though you're saying exactly the same thing.

When it comes to actual work, assignment comes first, then delegation. There is a difference. When you assign, you tell a person what you want done, how you want it done, and when you want it done. When you progress to the point of delegation, you are able to say, "What do you think should be done?" The person is experienced enough to start telling you.

Assignments have to be checked regularly, with work-in-process dates. Delegation needs only a completion date.

If you delegate too soon, you put a person in over his head. He could lose confidence. He could run into conflict with you as his boss. He could also lose respect within the organization. I've often seen it happen: somebody is brought in, put on the job, and abandoned. The leader expects him to figure out how to do it all alone. He doesn't always succeed.

Certain types of things should *never* be delegated to certain people. In business, for example, you never delegate expense accounts to salespeople. They seem to have a blind spot when it comes to spending money, entertaining, and so forth. You have to control that area yourself.

Other people can never really handle the freedom to work outside the office or have flexible hours. They'll start coming in later and later; somehow they lack the necessary personal discipline.

My personal philosophy, however, is to delegate everything I can, and only when that delegation has been neglected do I go back to making assignments. A lot rides on how I give the delegation in the first place. If I announced it with a lot of fanfare, the person loses face if it's pulled back. But if I can quietly say, "I believe we can improve this by both of us working on it," the person is usually spared the feeling he's going backwards.

Naturally, I don't like to get into this predicament. It's much better to delegate realistically in the first place.

All of this increases the assets of the organization. People are our greatest asset. Just as we improve a physical plant, we improve people. I'm as hesitant to fire somebody as I would be to burn down one of the buildings.

Seeing the Big Picture

Frequently, the person we are training has a job that fits into other jobs, but he doesn't really know how. In the meantime, he becomes a perfectionist. An educational director sometimes thinks the whole church operates just for the Sunday school. It's part of training to say how a job fits into the whole—not so much to increase the importance of that particular function as to build up the importance of other things.

Otherwise, people start developing little empires of their own that nobody else can break into. One department starts to operate independent of the rest. This is exactly what happens in the human body when cancer develops. A cell starts to operate independently, growing on its own without being coordinated with the rest of the cells.

I know a music minister who was fired because his Sunday morning music kept going too long, creeping into the sermon time—just half a minute at first, then a minute, two minutes, and finally more like five minutes. He was producing bigger and better numbers each week, or he would choose an offertory that far exceeded the time needed to take the offering. Once the music was underway, of course, what was the pastor to do but wait it out?

He talked to the music director and couldn't get him to control the length. In the end, believe it or not, he had to fire the man.

Whenever I'm with Cliff Barrows of the Billy Graham organization, even in the smallest meeting, I notice he always starts right on time. He has a sense of broadcast and telecast; he knows how ingredients fit into a total program.

For years I've also watched Cliff during Billy's sermons.

He's the most intense listener in the whole stadium. Cliff realizes he's up front, and any looking around or sleeping would depreciate the message.

Any staff member who sits in view of the congregation must accept his or her responsibility to the listeners. People on the platform ought to be the people who listen most; their endorsement of what is being said or sung is extremely important. The whole meeting is important, not just what one person does.

Five Criteria for Trainers

As training moves along, here are five ways to measure progress:

1. Is this person's job fitting well with his or her talents? If not, I haven't got a prayer of developing that person to his potential. He may have to do something temporarily that doesn't fit, but it's my responsibility over the long haul to see that the job and the talents match.

For example, you can't put a loner into a team operation. You may have a person who is irascible. You can't make an usher out of him.

2. How much willingness to do the job am I seeing? This goes beyond verbal expressions of "I really like this." I watch to see if the person is basically enthusiastic about opportunity, if this work is more than just something to fill the time. If I catch a sense of *Well, I'll do it if you want me to, but I'm not really keen on it,* I don't expect much. I want the person to have enough willingness to be enthusiastic.

3. How consistent is the person's effort? Sporadic effort is not what I want. Long-term, consistent, day-in day-out effort is what pays off in an organization.

You don't want someone who does things only when he feels like it. A friend told me one time, "The amateur performs well when he feels like it. The pro performs well whether he feels like it or not." Athletes talk about "playing hurt." The pro *expects* to play hurt. He doesn't call in sick. That's part of being a pro.

4. *What are the objective results?* A lot of people give you a lot of activity, conversation, excuses—but if you really measure what they've done, you find little. Some get by for years without really producing.

I know a fellow right now whom people talk highly of. Yet every time I've asked anyone specifically, "Tell me, what are you praising?" all I hear is "Oh, he's got personality. He's such a likable guy." But he's really never done much.

5. *Is this person willing to be evaluated?* I'm not going to spend time developing somebody who resists having his results measured. That, incidentally, is one of the problems I have with some educators today; they resist any kind of evaluation. It's not easy to evaluate a teacher, I admit, but it's not impossible.

Neither is it impossible to evaluate those we train in the church. This, too, is part of effective development.

NINE

MOTIVATING, NOT MANIPULATING

Leadership is getting people to work for you when they are not obligated to do so.

I recently heard a pastor tell about a wealthy oil man who called and said, "Reverend, I've never had much time for religion, but I'm getting older, and maybe I ought to make my peace with the church. I'd like to start by giving you a $20,000 check."

The preacher said, "I immediately extended to him the right hand of Christian fellowship."

I don't think he was joking.

The exchange was an example of manipulation, which despite being repudiated, still manages to find its way into the ministry. Why? Because it's effective—it just plain works! In this case, the church got a $20,000 windfall.

But manipulation comes with a price. The pastor manipulated the fellow into believing he was getting Christian fellowship, but the man also manipulated the preacher by buying his way in, which we all know is an impossible relationship.

By contrast, a young man named Philip makes films with Christian themes. He became acquainted with a non-Christian who shared his interest in film-making techniques but rejected the importance of personal commitment to Christ.

The non-Christian offered some valuable equipment, and

Philip said gently, "I appreciate the offer, but I can't accept unless you fully recognize that this gift does not get you any points with God. Your eternal destination is determined by your relationship with Christ, not whether you contribute to Christian films. Do you understand that?"

"I understand," the friend said.

"Then I'll accept the equipment."

Those two stories illustrate the difference between manipulation and motivation. Motivation is getting people to do something out of mutual advantage. Manipulation is getting people to do what you want them to do, primarily for *your* advantage. If the other person benefits, it's purely secondary.

Manipulation carries a hidden agenda. Motivation carries an open agenda. You can be totally honest with people.

The young film maker was saying, "Do we have enough mutual interest to get all the agenda on top of the table? I'm not going to manipulate you or let you manipulate me into a brownie point religion."

Walking the Fine Line

We all agree that motivation is good and manipulation is bad. But sometimes only a fine line separates the two, and it's difficult to know which side of the line you're on. The issues aren't always clear-cut—what may be a legitimate case of motivation in one situation could, with a different intent, be manipulation.

An example is a cook who hides eggplant, which you've said you'll never eat, in some kind of casserole. You say, "Hey, that's good. What is it?" Only then does he tell you. Were you manipulated? Or motivated?

A psychiatrist friend chided me one night by saying, "You businessmen mistake manipulation for motivation. The difference is you can substitute the word *thirst* for motivation but not manipulation." He was saying unless you are satisfying someone's thirst, you are probably manipulating rather than motivating. I've found that to be a good principle for distinguishing the two. I can motivate with integrity when I am bringing to consciousness a genuine thirst.

I was motivated in my appreciation of Dixieland music, for instance, by former Senator S. I. Hayakawa. He was an absolute authority on Dixieland, and we spent a pleasant evening discussing it. Later I realized that he, an excellent teacher and semanticist, had instilled a deeper interest than I'd had before.

He said, for example, "Cool jazz is courteous. Dixieland is discourteous because everybody talks at the same time. At the end of a number, after everybody's made a statement and they 'take it home,' everyone starts making a statement at the same time." He played on my intellectual interest to attract me to Dixieland.

He never said, "I'm going to try to intrigue you." He simply intrigued me.

Was that manipulation? I don't think so, because I already had some interest and he merely deepened it. Now I can listen to a band and tell which musicians are really making statements and which are just putting in time.

Whenever we try to motivate without the other person knowing what we are trying to do, however, we need to be careful. We can try to bring out a latent desire a person doesn't even know exists, but we need to remember three things: (1) Recognize how close we are to manipulation; (2) Set a checkpoint, and if the technique doesn't produce a genuine thirst, stop it; (3) Never resort to immoral means even for righteous ends.

A friend had a secretary who lived a free lifestyle with no apparent interest in the Christian way. One day a letter arrived from a student named Ed who closed with "Until I hear from you, I'll be floating around." My friend wrote him back, basically explaining how he could find spiritual reality without floating around. He rewrote that letter half a dozen times, not because he was dissatisfied with what he said the first time, but so it would have to be retyped by the secretary, who also was "floating around."

In a sense, that bordered on manipulation. But I feel (others may differ) that it was done with integrity, because my friend admitted to himself what he was doing, he ended it after a limited time, and his action did not exploit the woman—he was paying her a full salary for the typing.

Later he found she kept a copy of the letter for herself, and she eventually became a Christian. The process started with her typing that letter to Ed.

Instilling motivation is hard work. It takes a lot out of me to bring you where I want you to go. I sometimes hear people say, "Well, if a person doesn't want to go, I have no right to manipulate him to get him there." I may not have a right to manipulate, but neither can I allow the fear of manipulation to be a rationalization for not doing the hard work of instilling motivation, which is, after all, one of the leader's most important tasks.

At the same time, we limit anything that borders on manipulation because it is so easy to exploit people with it. To challenge people, to motivate with integrity, means I may put a lot of effort into a person, but the time comes when he must be set free. He may walk away and leave me empty-handed, but any more on my part would be dishonest manipulation. My only recourse is to start over with somebody else.

I once recommended a particular church to a young woman because she wanted to meet some sharp professional people. I sensed, however, that she wasn't very interested in spiritual things, so I didn't keep encouraging her to go. She would not have been going for the right reason. I simply wanted her to be exposed to the spiritual to see if there was any interest, to give the Spirit of God a chance to work. Apparently the time wasn't right, so I felt any more pushing would have been manipulation.

Uses and Abuses

In most cases, manipulation is the prostitution of motivation. Prostitution is always easier than the real thing; it's an attempt to get results without honest effort. Motivation is not a quick fix; manipulation can be.

A common example in the church is proof texting, where someone takes a promise people find very attractive (God wants you in a Rolls Royce) and digs up three or four Bible verses that say God will supply your deepest desire. That's manipulation, not honest instruction.

There are other ways we see manipulation in the church.

Appealing to human gratification. Anything that appeals primarily to human desire is manipulation; anything that satisfies divine desires is motivation.

If we structure a church so members come only to meet their human needs for friendship, security, belonging, or tradition, we are manipulating.

To find ways to motivate spiritually is difficult. It's much easier to find a human mutual interest than to implant a divine mutual interest. Divine interests may contradict human interests. If you decide church officers must fulfill the scriptural requirements for deacon or elder, think of the political fallout! In many cases, if you don't let the financially powerful exert their influence, they go to another church, or worse, wreak havoc in this one. So we manipulate by giving them human satisfactions: prestige, power, and authority in the congregation.

Flimsy assurances. Sometimes we satisfy people too easily—with meetings. One Christian woman I know quit attending missionary society meetings because she said they didn't do anything but meet, eat, and have a short prayer. The worst part, she said, was that everyone left feeling they had done something for missions when in fact they'd done nothing. The activity was manipulative—getting people to think they were working when they were actually just keeping busy.

Relying on recognition. I once talked with a young man who planned to give a large donation to establish a Christian institution.

"Are you doing this because God needs it?" I asked.

"Yes, I think so."

"Are you going to put your name on it?"

"Yes, I'd planned to."

"Then I don't think you're spiritually mature enough to do it," I said.

And he had the honesty to say, "That may be true. Maybe I'd better think about it for a while." Now, several years later, he's dropped the idea because his motivations have matured.

I could have simply suggested a contractor or an architect or a location or friends who could be involved. But that would have been manipulation. I wanted this young man to come to a spiritual motivation, and he has.

Selective appreciation. When a wealthy person gives a gift larger than other people but small compared to what he ought to give, exaggerated recognition for that gift is manipulative. It does not motivate.

Occasionally I see people recognized as outstanding leaders when the only outstanding thing they've done is to give more money than other people can afford. It hasn't affected their lives; it represented no sacrifice. Fawning over them is favoritism, which is condemned in Scripture.

Misuse of "ministry." I saw an ad on a seminary bulletin board for a secretarial job opening. It listed the normal skills required and then said, "Pay is low because it is a ministry." I wanted to tear it down.

I haven't the vaguest idea why a secretary working in a Christian setting should make less than a secretary in a secular setting. I understand even less how the location determines whether the secretary's job is a ministry.

I wouldn't mind if the ad had said, "We pay according to how much support we receive" or "Pay depends on how well the organization does financially." But to spiritualize low wages as "ministry" is manipulation.

These forms of manipulation are usually justified because they help the cause. But in the work of God, ends—even noble ends—never justify means. Such thinking humanizes God and eliminates his sovereignty. God becomes unnecessary as we presume to do for him what he couldn't do any other way. We forget God is as interested in the process by which we live as the product we produce. If that process is not divinely sanctioned, we are outside his will.

Means of Motivating

What are some motivational means? How can we bring out the best in people without resorting to manipulative tactics?

Establish a psychically friendly atmosphere. This is especially true with co-workers, whether volunteer or paid. In the corporate world, for instance, I'm very straightforward when hiring: I prefer "my kind of people"—people I can motivate. I can't motivate everybody. It's easier to manipulate than motivate. For long-term, day-to-day relationships, however, I need people I can motivate with integrity.

But when I've genuinely motivated someone, I can look him or her in the eye and know we have an honest, friendly relationship between us.

Enjoy people's uniqueness. Being friends is beneficial; having the same tastes is not necessary.

One young woman worked for me matching colors of ink. She could get tears in her eyes over certain shades of blue. "Isn't this a beautiful match?" she'd ask.

I never could figure what went on in her head to make matching blue such a remarkable occurrence. But all I needed to do to keep her motivated was to share her excitement and appreciate her work.

Know a person's capabilities. With this employee, the most unkind thing I could have done would have been to say, "Don't you ever think of anything more important than shades of blue?" The truth of the matter was, more often than not, she didn't. Nor would my criticism have made her a better person. She was helping the company by doing what she enjoyed.

I must spend time to know what a person can do. My responsibility is to make as objective an evaluation as I can of present skills, potential capacities, level of commitment, ability to be motivated, discipline, and intensity. If I am to lead, I owe it to my people to take the time to evaluate well.

The key is not to let feelings override judgment. I try to be as objective with a person as I am with money. If I count your money, the fact that I like you won't make me adjust the bottom line. I need to be just as objective about your ability, drive, and dedication.

My color matcher didn't have extensive capabilities, and to motivate her above her capacity would have been cruel. If a musician has limited talent, it's a sin to talk about the joys of being a Mozart. When you're with a woman who is single at age fifty-five, you don't overdo motherhood. In motivation, desire must be matched with ability. You focus on the advantages of being who you are and not what somebody else is.

The greatest demotivator is to say, "Do you ever think about what you could have been?" How cruel! Motivation always looks to the future.

Know how much responsibility a person can take. Some people can take sizable responsibility but not sole responsibility. They may have great abilities, but something in their psyche says, *I don't want the whole load. I want somebody to lean on, to report to.*

Some people work best with assignments rather than responsibility. Assignments mean you explain what you want, when you want it, and how you want it done. Responsibility means the person takes initiative and gets the job done effectively by whatever means he or she develops.

Good leaders know which kind of people are working for them.

Look for ways both of you can benefit. A certain honesty is required in motivation. It admits that unless there is a mutual interest, perhaps we shouldn't get involved in this thing together.

If a person does have potential, a good question to ask is: "You have a lot more talent than you've been able to put to use. How much effort are you willing to exert if we give you the opportunity to develop that talent?"

The development, of course, has to be in line with the ministry. I wouldn't invest church resources to train somebody who wanted to be a watchmaker. We have to find the mutual advantage. But we can be looking for individuals who want to develop certain skills from which the church can benefit. When a person sees he or she is improving in some area, and it is also helping the body, this is a powerful motivation.

Be honest about your goals. A young minister came to see me not long ago. He wanted to know how he could build his small church into a big church.

"What's your primary motivation?" I asked.

"Frankly, the size church I've got can't pay me enough to live on," he said.

For him to begin an evangelism program, he would have to manipulate people. He couldn't be honest about it.

His church was big enough to support a pastor if he could convince them to tithe, but he'd rather go into a church expansion program than try to teach people to tithe.

Use people as positive illustrations. In my speaking, I've told how certain people excelled at something, perhaps a Christian virtue. They seemed to love it—and began to exhibit even more of those positive traits. This becomes manipulation only if what you're saying is untrue or slanted—or if you threaten to use a person as a bad illustration.

One of the ways I motivate people to think is always to carry some blank cards in my pocket, and when anyone says something worth writing down, I do so. For years I tried to remember memorable lines until I was alone and could jot myself a note. Then I overheard someone say, "I didn't know it was that good, but he wrote it down!" I realized people love to be quoted. And quoting them motivates them to think better.

Now in conversation I'll often say, "May I write that down?" It has excellent motivating power.

One of the nicest compliments you can earn is "He makes me think smart when I'm with him." It's a sign you are motivating people to think.

Give a person a reputation to uphold. One of my bosses had a way of saying nice things about his workers that got back to them. True things but nice things. We appreciated it, and we couldn't keep from trying to do more things he could tell. People will work hard to uphold a good reputation.

Ask *What is special about this person?* For example, some people rarely say anything negative. That's a beautiful reputation to start giving them. "Here's a person who looks for the best in people." Of course, you can't be dishonest and say that about a cynic.

I have consciously augmented my wife's reputation as a creative listener. She is. I did it basically to comfort her because she'd always say after a social occasion, "I didn't have anything to say. All I did was listen." And yet, she does that better than anyone I know.

One night at a dinner party, she was sitting next to a quiet, powerful man. His wife, sitting next to me, said, "I feel sorry for your wife having to sit next to Jack."

"Jack will talk his head off," I said.

"You don't know Jack."

"No," I replied, "but I know my wife."

Jack talked his head off. I'm sure his wife thought, *What in the world happened to Jack?* It was simple—Mary Alice has the ability to listen dynamically, to make people feel they're smart. And often they live up to it!

Compliment with credibility. I learned a secret of complimenting from Sarah Jarman, an intelligent, impeccable woman. Her compliments were never general, always specific. "That tie and that suit are exactly right for each other." From then on, I'd wear that tie with that suit.

It was obvious her observations were well thought out, believable, and correct. She never tried to compliment you on something outside her field of expertise. She understood social graces, and the thing she knew best she would compliment you on. She was believable.

I never will forget talking with a professional singer after a concert, and a lady came up and gushed, "You sure did sing well."

The singer thanked her, but after she left, he said, "I could spit."

"Why?" I asked.

"That woman doesn't know how poorly or how well I sang. All she knows is whether or not I made her feel good. I know she meant well, but I wish she'd just said, 'I enjoyed your singing,' rather than rendering a judgment on something she knows little about."

Compliments mean the most when you know what you're talking about.

Show people you enjoy your work. I learned from my former boss, Maxey Jarman, that it was fun to work.

One time, half complaining and fishing for praise, I said, "I sure am working hard."

Maxey replied, "What would you rather be doing?"

"Nothing," I had to admit.

"Then," said he matter-of-factly, "you shouldn't complain about doing what you'd rather do."

By observing him and seeing how grateful he was for his responsibility, I realized I liked to work. That's when I had the most fun and satisfaction.

A friend once said, "I was a sophomore at Princeton before I realized it was fun to learn. Then school became exciting." He was fortunate. That doesn't happen to a lot of students until it's too late.

I don't have a higher education, but one of the blessings is that I never learned to study for grades. My friends in higher education have confirmed that those who learned to study for grades are often delayed as thinkers. They say the B students in seminary will often be the best pastors.

(Then, tongue in cheek, they say the A students come back as professors and administrators—and they usually wind up calling on the C students for money, because they've become the money makers.)

Finding Thirsty People

If the difference between motivation and manipulation is the quenching of thirst, then the key for a leader is to look for thirsty people.

People, however, have different thirsts, and to motivate them means knowing their thirsts. Viktor Frankl has taught us that almost everyone has a basic thirst for meaning in life. There are other thirsts: worthwhile accomplishment, utilization of talents, approval of God. One of the greatest for those in Christian work is a thirst to belong, a desire for community in the kingdom of God.

One of the secrets of identifying a person's thirst is to see what has motivated him or her in the past. People rarely outlive their basic thirst. If they get a thirst young in life, they seldom lose it. If they have a thirst for recognition, these people never seem to get quite enough fame. If they thirst for intellectual growth, they never get quite smart enough. If they want money, I rarely see them get to the point where they don't want more.

Then, once we've identified where people are dry, effective motivators ask themselves, *What kind of water do I have to satisfy that kind of thirst?*

When we are able to honestly and openly offer water to parched people, we are not manipulating. We are motivating.

T E N

FROM PREACHING TO COMMUNICATING

Vision, policies, and plans are more or less useless unless they are known to all who may be concerned with them. Lord Montgomery, commander of the Eighth Army, made it a rule that the plan of the campaign should be made known to every soldier.

Preaching will forever remain at the core of the church's program. Along with teaching, preaching is one of the chief sources of spiritual power. Any attempt to reduce its importance is, in my opinion, a dead-end street.

The message of preaching forever remains the same, but the form changes to successfully reach the hearers, just as the Bible itself has been retranslated in our time to great advantage. I was once given a framed page from the Geneva Bible of 1560—and I can't read it. It is the Word of God, all right, but its form is such that modern people cannot easily understand it.

One of the most significant developments in the church today, as I see it, is that old-style "preaching" is going out, and "communication" is coming in. Those preachers who have adjusted to the change in people's listening habits and interests are having no trouble drawing a crowd; they're able to match the gospel with current needs. (Certain legendary preachers will not change, and do not need to change. They became who they are in another generation. But they cannot be imitated successfully today.)

How the Ears Have Changed

This need for change has been brought on by several concurrent happenings, one of which is our transformation into a society of television watchers.

TV has conditioned us to getting information quickly in short blasts, "capsules." In the dramas, a whole life situation is developed and solved in thirty minutes or an hour. In the newscasts, world issues are given a couple minutes, and authorities are asked to sum up "in the thirty seconds we have left."

So audiences expect quick analysis, direct answers. About the only place people listen to a lecture is at church, and they are less equipped, less willing, and less able to receive extensive information in this form. Preachers who want to communicate cannot completely ignore this.

Television is also an intimate medium. The camera zooms in close and makes things very personal. Viewers have learned to watch for subtle expressions rather than grand gestures.

That's what got Frank Clements, the governor of Tennessee a generation ago, crossed up when he delivered the opening speech at a Democratic convention. People called him "cornpone" afterward. But H. V. Kaltenborn, then the dean of news reporting, who did not see Clements on television but heard him in the convention hall, said it was one of the greatest political speeches he had ever heard. On a platform or in an open field, all of his magnified gestures and raised voice would have been natural. But when the camera came bearing down on his face, it made him look corny.

In addition, television has tended to portray preachers as arm-waving Elmer Gantrys. Theatrical preaching is lampooned. When people see it used in church, no matter how sincere the preacher may be, they sense it is not completely believable. It doesn't seem real to a generation accustomed to the poise of a network anchorman.

As I visit churches, I'm amazed how many preachers still

shout, even with microphones available. I went to a church not long ago with no more than a hundred people, and the pastor was screaming. I said to myself, *What is he saying that demands yelling?* I took some of his points and repeated them to myself quietly—and they weren't bad! He could have been so much more effective with that audience by saying things in a normal volume. But by habit, he didn't think he was preaching until he had raised his voice, stomped the floor, and kicked the pulpit.

It is not only the media that have decreased the respect for "old-time preaching," but also the changing moral environment of our society. There was a time when preachers, like doctors, were automatically respected. Today, people do not automatically say, "The preacher is right and I am wrong." They do not see sin as bad and faith as good. No longer is the Bible the moral dictionary for most people. Right and wrong have become confused. Preachers are often seen as caricatures.

Some of the damage has been self-inflicted by preachers wanting to be thought of as "one of the boys." It is comfortable but damaging for ministers to get up in the pulpit and talk, without restraint, about their weaknesses and doubts rather than their beliefs and hope. God has called preachers to a unique office, one that we dare not belittle.

Fulton Sheen once chastised those priests and nuns who wanted to be an "equal among equals." He castigated them for giving up their power of "substitutionary grace." While Protestants might not accept that theologically, they cannot avoid Paul's willingness to say, "Follow me as I follow Christ."

Another part of the modern depreciation has to do with the image the electronic church is creating. The cost of TV is so high that, of necessity, television preachers spend a great deal of time raising money. Therefore the unchurched tend to think preaching means money grubbing.

Malcolm Muggeridge once said television is not a good medium for spreading the gospel because it is essentially an entertainment medium. I think he is right. Newscasters rec-

ognize the entertainment factor—and so do most TV preachers. The ratings influence programming, which puts pressure
on television preachers to be ever more dramatic and overly
dynamic. This, too, tends to make people question their
sincerity.

What we need today are preachers who can go onto a
platform and be believable and persuasive—an example of
God's power. We are coming into a time when people will be
most influenced by *communicators*, not by "preachers," at least
those who persist in the old form of three points and a poem
delivered with a seminary brogue or an unnatural tone of
voice.

Three Kinds of Communicators

The preachers and teachers I hear divide into three general
categories: orators, speakers, and talkers. Effective communicators select the style that fits their personality and develop it
into a consistently high skill.

• *Orators.* Few of these are left. Oratory demands the soul
of a poet and the articulation of a great actor. Orators love
ideas and design artistic phrases to properly attire them. They
have the ability to present them dramatically without artifici-
ality. Few individuals are noble enough by nature to be orators. There is something celestial about oratory. I wish I could
do it, but I can't.

I found that out in the middle of one of my first oratorical
efforts. I suddenly stopped and told the audience, "Folks, I
am not an orator, but I read a book on it, and I was so inspired
that I tried it, and you've just seen me prove I can't do it. Now
if you'll just let me talk to you, I promise never to try that
again." And I haven't.

Unfortunately, I hear a great many preachers who were
taught the basic skills of oratory, and from that egg has
hatched an ugly gosling—an awkward, unreal caricature,
owning all the disadvantages of oratory with few, if any, of
the advantages.

Oratory, like grand opera, has a very limited audience and fewer capable performers. Or, to use another metaphor, oratory is a pocket watch in a wrist watch world.

I once met a young country preacher before a Sunday service. To my amazement, as soon as he walked into the pulpit, he changed his voice tone, tempo, and body actions. He delivered a badly beat-up oration that sounded like a poor impersonation of R. G. Lee. No one had told him how disastrous it is to imitate the unique. He would have been much better using his own style.

● *Speakers.* The speaker has a subject and an outline with understandable points, well illustrated, including some one-liners people can take home with them. The illustrations are from life, proving to the listeners that the speaker lives in the same world they do, faces the problems and sees the difficulties they see. They find answers they can use.

Speakers such as Chuck Swindoll, Dick Halverson, James Dobson, Howard Hendricks, and Charles Colson consistently rate high on religious radio surveys. These are the communicators most young preachers and teachers should emulate. It is not easy, however, because seminaries traditionally have not taught this style of communication.

● *Talkers.* A talker (and I'm one) is a lazy speaker—at least that's what a great many people think. I, of course, would differ. To me, it is more difficult to be a talker than a speaker, for a speaker decides what he is going to say and sticks to it.

Talkers are more conversational, do not use a formal outline, and yet the good ones know exactly what they are trying to accomplish. They pause and talk to individuals in the audience. Everything seems extemporaneous, and the power of the style is that people do not see any art or structure. Therefore they are not distracted from the message itself.

Most often, good talkers carry two or three messages in their mind and adjust as their radar senses what the audience is receiving and understanding. Using fewer dynamics and dramatics, the talker doesn't develop the verbal momentum the speaker or orator does.

For example, Arthur Godfrey was a talker. He was believable, informal, personal—the kind of person you would like as a friend. Will Rogers was a talker. Hugh Downs and David Hartman also have the talker's personality.

Although there are differences in style between talkers, speakers, and orators, the dedication and necessary degree of preparation is the same. Only the *kind* of preparation is different.

For anyone who decides to be an orator—and I'm not saying you should not, even after pointing out the difficulties and the lack of general interest—I must admit I cannot offer much help. I only warn: you had better be great, or you will be terrible.

On the other hand, for those wanting to be a speaker or talker, here's a format that has been helpful to me.

1. Select a strong single idea.

2. Give it a handle, a one-liner, so people can carry it home.

3. Illustrate it so they will remember it and apply it to themselves.

4. If necessary, extrapolate from the idea to the principle. (Too much extrapolation, however, becomes condescension. If you have a good idea with a good handle and illustration, most people will get the principle.)

For instance, here are the elements of a talk I gave last week:

The idea: *Live today so as to make tomorrow better.*

The one-line handle: *"Don't make a junkyard of your old age."*

The illustration: A young man who walks out on his family is giving up his children and his grandchildren in his old age. He is giving up memories of life shared. He's taking on the guilt of irresponsibility.

I spelled these out in some detail. I didn't need to extrapolate: "Are you ever tempted to live for the moment . . . to make a junkyard out of your old age? Do you ever feel like taking your savings and blowing it all on one good time? Are you ever tempted to get into dope or escape into alcohol? These are the ways we make junkyards out of our old age."

None of this was necessary; the handle and illustration had done the work.

Addressing People, Not a Subject

Whether speakers or talkers, we must think of what our listeners need to hear, not what we need to say. Our material should not be an expression of egotism, our "much learning," or the things people have complimented. Our content should grow out of a careful analysis of the needs of the listeners. I try to remind myself I'm speaking to people, not to a subject.

That may sound purely semantic. But many preachers are authorities on a subject without being authorities on the audience. They feel they have communicated whether the listeners got anything or not.

During World War II, when we needed to train technical people very quickly, we had a program called Training Within Industry (TWI). One of the basic tenets was "The teacher hasn't taught until the student has learned." If an applicant for a welding job went through TWI and came out unable to weld, we didn't blame the student; we blamed the teacher.

As communicators, if people don't get what we say, it's our fault, not theirs. Our job is to influence the thinking and actions of the people who hear us. I am not relieved of my responsibility just by enunciating syllables to show my knowledge of the Word. I have succeeded only when they understand and apply the scriptural principles.

I used to do some professional speaking with Norman Vincent Peale at chambers of commerce and other civic meetings. I asked him one time, "How do you decide what to speak on?"

He said, "On Friday I ask myself, 'What is the most common problem I've run into this week?' That helps me to decide." He was talking to people, not to subjects. No wonder he's been so popular throughout his long career.

A misconception has gotten into a lot of preachers, based perhaps on something Ralph Waldo Emerson said: "If a man can write a better book, preach a better sermon, or make a better mousetrap than his neighbor, though he builds his house in the woods, the world will make a beaten path to his door." That's just one of the foolish things out of Emerson's mouth. It's basically Eastern philosophy—the guru out on a mountaintop, and people trudging out to hear him.

A lot of empty churches have proven Emerson was wrong. Even Jesus said, "Go into all the world." He didn't say, "Sit here, and the world will come to you." One of our problems, I think, is that we have built a fishpond (the baptistery) and then invited the fish to come in and swim. It has not been the nature of fish to do that. We will have a lot more success if we go out to the lake, *their* natural habitat.

I used to get up at five in the morning and go to Lake Barkley in western Kentucky to listen to the fishermen. I like to be among enthusiastic people, even if they're doing something I think is strange. Here were perfectly intelligent people getting up at four in the morning to be at the lake by five. Why? Because that's when the fishing was the best. They were even buying night crawlers and red worms. Why? Because that's what fish like to eat.

I doubt if fish would really go for steak. But I see Christians all the time trying to use bait *they* like. We have to ask, "What will the unbelievers be attracted to?" We don't prostitute the gospel, but we change its form to make it attractive.

If the class I substitute-teach were suddenly to drop from seven hundred to one hundred, I would not feel righteous for giving them "the pure Word" and blame them for not listening. I would say, "I have apparently lost contact with these people and their problems."

A singles group asked me to do a retreat: five lectures of two hours each, followed by discussion. I got there and realized what I had prepared was not the most useful thing for them. I didn't deliver a single one of those lectures.

Instead, we had a tremendous amount of dialogue. Then I'd go back to my room and stay up half the night synthesizing what we'd talked about so I could bring it back in a cogent form the next session. I left there wobbling on my feet because I hadn't had any sleep. But I got a lot of reaction from those people saying, "This was one of the most meaningful experiences of my life." I was dealing with their problems, taking what knowledge I have of scriptural principles and applying it to their current needs.

One woman at that retreat, a successful interior decorator, wrote me later: "I delayed writing you because I had decided at our session to do three things. I wanted to be sure I had done them before I told you."

Nothing pleases me more than that.

Principles, Not Prooftexts

Sometimes we get superstitious about Bible words, as if they had special power. That's why some of us were slow to change from the King James Version. If we gave up that particular combination of words, what might happen?

The principles are immutable. They are the way God runs this world. As long as we don't violate the principles but make them applicable to people in a form they can understand and put into practice, we are communicating God's truth.

Not long ago, I was speaking to a business group on "how a Christian takes loss." By eight o'clock the next morning, the president of a company was in my office asking how I would like to lose several million dollars, file for bankruptcy, and have to move my wife out of our home.

I assured him that was not a high set of items on my priority list. I asked if that was his situation.

"Yes," he said. "I heard you talk about loss, and I want to talk about mine."

It would have been easy to escape my responsibility by giving him a few verses of Scripture, offer to put him on my prayer list, then slap him on the back and walk him to the elevator. That would also have been hypocrisy.

I spent an hour and a half with him, going through his options. We discovered some he had forgotten. A major loss casts a shadow over us, and often at these times, we need someone else to help us plan a way through the confusion.

Finally I said, "Don't interpret this loss as the judgment of God, because he's not as interested in your success as your maturity."

Now I could have backed all this up with verses of Scripture, but that wasn't what he needed. He needed the *principles* of Scripture, and he needed someone to help him apply them. I don't feel I have a right to speak to people about solutions that I'm not willing to help them apply.

Making the Message Clear

The great communicators are great illustrators. I realize some preachers are sensitive about storytelling. Once at a ministers' meeting, I was urging the move from old-time preaching to communication, and a young man came up afterward and said, "I would like to be more effective—but I've listened to those famous communicators you named, and all they do is tell stories."

I replied, "Isn't that what Jesus did?"

"Yeah, I guess so," he said, rather reluctantly.

Jesus illustrated mainly from current happenings. He didn't tell a lot of Bible stories—which comes as a great surprise to many people. His illustrations *became* Bible stories after he told them.

We don't need to limit ourselves to his stories to convey the truth. We need to take the truth he conveyed and put it into believable, current illustrations.

The Sunday morning class I frequently guest-teach has a lot of sophisticated, highly successful Dallas people. Not long after the Southern Baptist Convention had been in town, I told them the story of a large Christian meeting that was held downtown at the Hilton. The chairman came out of his room a little bit late to get the program started. He discovered a guy had been mugged in the hall, and he stood there a minute trying to decide whether to stop and help, which would mean delaying the convention, or . . . he finally concluded his platform responsibility was primary, so he rushed ahead.

Out of a room on the other side of the hall came one of the official messengers, anxious to get downstairs for the opening. He saw the guy who had been mugged, but since he was representing a large church, he really needed to be at the meeting.

Then along came a nonbeliever who took the guy to the hospital. He told the hotel manager that in a few days, this fellow would be better and would be checking back into the hotel. He would leave his American Express charge open so that if the fellow didn't have adequate credit, they could just add the expenses to his account.

Now obviously, that was nothing but the Good Samaritan story. I went on from there to say, "The question of this story is not 'What occupation do I have?' It doesn't mean you're supposed to go patrol the halls of downtown hotels looking for people who've been mugged.

"What this story is about is defining who is a neighbor. A neighbor is anyone who provides you and me an opportunity to do good."

Such stories, I realize, are not looked upon with favor in some preaching circles. Some Christians feel the "offense of the Cross" means we don't try to make the gospel attractive or interesting. I disagree.

My responsibility as a communicator is to get as many people to hear as much of the gospel as I possibly can. It isn't my responsibility to run people away. I could do that by just not having the meeting.

Being Sincere and Personal

Two of the most important traits of a communicator are sincerity and the ability to establish a one-to-one atmosphere quickly.

One of my friends, who has developed persuasion into an art, told me, "The most important thing in selling is to be sincere. The other person must believe *you* believe what you're saying, even though *he* may not believe what you're saying."

Sincerity goes all the way from dress and manners to preparation and presentation. Audiences can read a speaker's integrity. Sometimes in front of a crowd, I will change my material just to be sure I don't say anything I don't feel. If I were scheduled to do an inspirational talk and I didn't feel inspired, I wouldn't get up and prove it. I would change my attitude or my material.

Closely related to sincerity is learning to go one-to-one with the audience as quickly as possible. I do not want to be a speaker and them a mass audience. I want us to be friends.

John Stein, the great impresario, told me the common denominator of successful platform personalities is that people quickly feel they are persons, not performers. I notice how quickly Billy Graham does this even in a large stadium. He will say something like "You are not here by accident. You are here by the will of God." Immediately he is one-to-one with them. They are no longer anonymous.

I've never heard worse advice than to tell a speaker to look a foot above the audience's heads. That's fine—if you're speaking to the wall. Your words will bounce right back to you.

Using Your Radar

Radar is the ability to discern what's really happening in an audience through their unintended cues—the noise level, the changing expressions, the movement of heads in agreement or disagreement.

If you have no radar, then you must decide what topic you want to treat, write down your remarks, deliver them, and hope for the best. I assure you, communicators do more than this.

You want to start using your radar before you get up to speak. I often start by arriving early, before the crowd does, so I can watch them choose their seats. If people fill up the back, they're expecting a sermon. If they sit up front, they're expecting a show. At church the cheap seats are up front; at a theater they're in the back. That's just human nature: If something's going to be "good for you," you get as far away as you can. If it's going to be entertaining, you get as close as you can. It helps me to know what the audience is anticipating.

I also like to listen to the noise level of a group before they're seated. A group of accountants makes very little noise. A group of salesmen makes a lot. You also can tell whether the group enjoys one another—are they homogeneous as they move around, or are they in little groups?

I spoke at a large deacons' meeting not long ago where before the meeting, the older deacons were all standing around talking to each other, with the young deacons standing "afar off." I asked one of the older men, "Do you know the younger deacons?"

He said, "No, and I'm not going to try to know them."

That was important information for me as I spoke!

Another important clue is what people laugh at and the quality of their laughter. A psychiatrist and I sat together during one speech, and suddenly he nudged me and said, "Listen to the hollow laughter." People were laughing courteously, the way kids laugh (or even groan) at puns.

It pays to watch *who* laughs. Not everyone does. If you get only the old-timers to laugh, you'd better find something pretty soon to give the younger people before you lose them. One of the most wonderful preachers I know has lost all appeal to young people, and his audience is getting older and older. He's going to have a real problem soon, because the old-timers won't be around long. It's young people who fill the nursery.

Beyond laughter, I watch for any point that gets a reaction. Women generally react more openly than men. But if you start compromising yourself just for reaction, doing the sentimental things that many women react to, the men will soon turn you off, and you'll be talking to the Women's Missionary Society. So if you do something sentimental, remember to do something a little tougher, too. Everybody should leave the meeting having gotten at least one thing. If they don't, they will question whether they ought to come back. They may come back for ritualistic purposes, but they won't listen when they do.

While reading noises and movements, of course, you can't be bothered by one or two deadpan people. Some deadpans are listening intently. One of the worst mistakes I ever made while giving a talk was to let one person irritate me. I got to talking to that one person and forgot the audience. Even if one person goes to sleep, that's not bad. (Now if they're sleeping all over the audience, that's another story.)

I like to watch people who take notes and see if they're taking notes at the right places. You see a lot of people who don't know how; they're writing down the wrong thing, and you want to stop and say, "Hey buddy, you missed the real point!" (Of course, then he might say, "I wasn't listening; I was doing my income tax.")

How is it possible to use your "radar" and still keep your actual words coming out straight? It's like learning to drive a car. The first time you sit behind the wheel, you're over-whelmed with instructions: Stay in the lane, don't ride the clutch, remember your turn signals, don't jam the brakes all at once. . . . But before long, you drive with all the ease in the world—and you read the highway signs to boot. It has become second nature.

The mind is capable of doing fantastic things once we get interested in developing it. A speaker ought always to be reaching out, increasing sensitivity, awareness, calculation powers. There isn't anything like hard work to make a good speaker. When I speak, it's nothing for me to spend forty to fifty hours on one address. The audience has no idea; when it looks effortless, they think it's extemporaneous.

Jackie Robinson playing second base had a marvelous abil-ity to relax. You'd think he was asleep, but when the ball came his way, or he was running the bases, you found out differently. Art should always appear effortless. But it takes effort to appear effortless.

How to Use Humor

Humor should be used to sharpen the truth, not to dull it. Humor should never help people *escape* from a truth; it's easy to let people off the hook.

How can humor dull the truth? Here's an example: "Yes, we're all sinners—but how else could we enjoy life?" That remark would be buying a cheap laugh at the cost of an important point. The crowd would laugh—but there's an old saying, "While the audience laughed, the angels cried." That's one of my tests of appropriate humor: Do the angels laugh too?

I'm not a very good joke teller. Instead, I use situational humor. Jokes make you a comedian; situational humor makes you a Will Rogers. He had the ability to use humor to set up points. He did not dull them. I prefer to have the doctor lubricate the needle before he sticks me. That's what humor can do: lubricate the needle.

Good humor ought to be like good spice, permeating the whole. I object to a speaker who uses humor only at the opening of a talk. When I speak, I'm never more serious than when I'm humorous, because I am firmly convinced I can say almost anything with humor if I work at it.

It's true that some people have a greater gift for humor. But nothing is more attractive to an audience than somebody who has the humility of humor. A wealthy young businessman who's developing a national reputation asked me about public speaking, and I said, "Tell stories."

He said, "My ego wouldn't let me."

That's what keeps a lot of people from using humor. They want to seem heavy, profound. Others view humor as a high-risk venture; what if the punch line bombs? That, incidentally, is why I practice any major piece of humor on several friends before I ever use it in public.

For example, I said to my rather affluent class the other Sunday, "I'm very depressed today. . . ." (Normally I'm not depressed, and they know it. I also don't believe in using an audience for my own therapeutic purposes. I'm there for them; they're not there for me. So I wasn't complaining.)

"I guess the reason I'm depressed is that Mary Alice and I just got back from two weeks in a very posh Colorado resort. And I realized I was the only one there with a green American Express card.

"Do you know how embarrassing that is? All my friends had gold or platinum. It was just so hard to feel good about yourself. I mean, how are you going to impress a waiter with a green card? When it came time to pay the bill, I found myself hiding my card with my napkin. . . ."

While I built up the spoof, they were laughing, but they were also thinking: *That's one of my problems, isn't it?* I could have stood up and preached against materialism and comparing ourselves with our neighbors, but they wouldn't really have heard me. Humor made the point much better.

But I had to practice that parody on several friends in private conversation, to see how they responded, before I ever used it on an audience.

The Power of the Parenthesis

There's more effect than most people think in "the power of the parenthesis." People tend to believe parenthetical remarks because they seem extemporaneous.

That's why I never say to an audience, "Last night when I was talking on this subject. . . ." That makes the listeners feel they're getting something warmed over. They start listening to my words as a speech, not a communication.

Instead, tremendous results can come from inserting things that seem off the subject but really aren't.

For example, before one crowd I said, almost as an aside, "I came home tired the other night, ate dinner, sat down, went to sleep, and woke up just feeling terrible. It was one of those nights when I would have had two big belters if I were a drinking man. But I guess I'm old enough to know drinking just causes problems—it doesn't solve them."

I dropped that remark because one of the big problems in that group is social drinking. They're under constant pressure at parties. Some of them may just be waiting for a rationale to refrain. (I remember talking to an executive who drank because everybody else did. When he asked me why I didn't, I said, "Because I have a right not to drink." He had never thought of it as a *right*, and he stopped drinking as a result.)

These asides can be more effective than making a full-blown point. The truth seems unthreatening, it catches people off guard, and I've found that for some strange reason, they remember it longer.

This is why I could never *read* a speech. I might as well send it in the mail. I'd lose the personal feedback, the eye contact, the body language, and especially the opportunity to throw in parentheses.

We do these things in conversation all the time. You may be talking to someone about a business matter, and you say, "That reminds me of something that happened at our house the other night." It's a little psychological break, a breather. The mind can handle this as well as keep track of the main subject.

In fact, the main subject often proceeds better after that, because you're relaxed. Sometimes I even say, "Excuse me for that little diversion." But I sense people appreciate the diversion if it makes sense.

The Joyful Debt

I still get as excited about *preparing* a speech as I did years ago. I'm not as excited about *giving* it these days, because I've spoken so much.

I have a little saying by which I test myself occasionally:

"You're not ready to speak for God until, after preparing, you'd rather have somebody else speak."

One of my friends said, "That lets me out." I know the feeling, but I stand by my test.

When a pastor says, "I don't mind standing up in front of people; preparation is what kills me," I suspect he's not a communicator as much as he is an exhibitionist.

When you realize every person in the audience is giving you thirty to sixty minutes of their lives, the numbers get pretty big. I'm humbled at the number of human hours I'm responsible for. I *owe* them something. Even small crowds deserve my best.

I hate to admit this, but it's true: Most audiences are not expecting much. They haven't gotten much in the past, and they're not anxious for you to start talking. You may be nervous, but they're not.

If you give them something a little exciting, new or helpful, they will appreciate it. They got more than they expected. And they'll probably be back to hear you next time.

ELEVEN

POINTING TOWARD MATURITY

To tackle problems in a masterly way, the leader must see things whole as well as in separate parts.

While I was speaking at a church in Cincinnati, a visitor from India walked by the auditorium and heard me. He took a seat in the back.

On Monday morning, he called to ask if we could meet for lunch. I discovered this man was a Ph.D. in chemistry and a devoted follower of Gandhi.

I asked, "What have you observed about Americans?"

"Well," he said, "you Americans are segmented. A large segment of your life is devoted to making money. You have another segment for family, another for social interaction, and yet another segment for religion. But they're not tied together with any philosophical thread. Each of them stands alone, almost as if you are a different person in each of these roles."

"Tell me about Dr. Gandhi," I asked.

"Dr. Gandhi had all the areas of interest I have just mentioned, but in his life, each was an expression of his religion."

I realized this chemist had made a profound observation about American life. I also realized his comment about Gandhi was one of the greatest compliments I had ever heard paid to a person. The focused, unsegmented life is a rarity today.

Even the church, at least in our culture, sometimes has a

tendency to segment persons. We take the segment of a person's life called "spiritual" and dress it up differently from the rest. We bring the person into a different culture on Sunday, seat him with people he may not see during the week, and use a peculiar vocabulary. All this has little to do with his job at the canning factory or computer terminal. Few people think of their business as an expression of their religion. Few think about time spent with family as a religious act, or social occasions as religious experiences.

This segmentation is something even the best-intentioned leaders fall into.

After speaking at a seminary chapel service, I met with the faculty, and the first question someone asked was, "How long have you been bivocational?"

"What do you mean?" I asked.

The person said, "How long have you had a ministry as well as a business?"

"I'm not bivocational," I said. "That term suggests one interest is above the other, or that I stop doing one temporarily while I'm doing the other. That's not so; I carry them simultaneously. Hopefully I am a whole person—a Christian. Both my speaking and my business are expressions of that wholeness."

I could tell even these sophisticated professors had a segmented concept of the Christian life.

I once saw William F. Buckley talking to Malcolm Muggeridge on television. Buckley said, "I would find it very difficult to talk to my compatriots about anything spiritual."

Muggeridge replied, "I find it difficult not to."

Obviously, Buckley accepts compartmentalization. He is brilliant, articulate, attends mass regularly, and is ready to write or get on national television and talk about spirituality— but not in normal conversation.

The ultimate goal of a church leader, as I see it, is to lead people to maturity in Christ. This, of course, starts with their salvation, which opens the possibility of maturing the saved.

And what is maturity if not living an integrated, consistent life? Maturing Christians are people who are becoming less and less compartmentalized. All of life is an expression of their faith.

The Consistent Christian Life

When I go to a religious retreat, I get the uneasy feeling some people are trying to fulfill their religious obligation all at one time. It's almost like children forced to eat spinach—they stall around, then gulp it down in one huge bite to get it over. Or like paying an insurance premium annually—one large effort, and it's taken care of for the year.

For two or three days, retreatants are willing to talk about their faith. But if you ask, "How would you like to do this next week?" they'd say, "Heavens, no. We've done enough."

A mature faith is homogenized. I'm very impressed with the approach of one church that offers a program called "Growth" one Saturday a month, and laymen have a chance to consider their total lives. One time they talk about investments, for instance. Another morning, they'll discuss ambition or office politics. They're making an attempt to homogenize faith and life, and to me, that's a step toward maturity.

Spiritual leaders lead toward that consistent Christian life. They deal with all areas, not just the spiritual. They address not just family devotions but family discipline and decision making. They emphasize not just the tithe but the whole concept of money making from a Christian perspective. Mature Christians understand the difference, for instance, between materialism and living in a material world. I find lots of Christians, even church staff people, who spend too much time thinking about the money their chosen profession does not provide. Thinking too much about money is materialism, whether you have money or not.

Another area for integration rather than segmentation is our relationship with non-Christians. These should be friendly, focusing on what we share in common, not continually pointing out how different we are.

The apostle Paul commands us not to be "conformed to this world" but "transformed by the renewing of your minds." Sometimes we find it more comfortable simply to shun non-Christians than to say, "When you're right, I'm going to join you. If you're wrong, I am going to call it to your attention as inoffensively as I can, or at least not participate." If we are conformed to the world's values, we never have freedom. But if we are transformed, we have freedom to be redemptive, and all our relationships can be redemptive. That's maturity.

Yesterday I was listening to a pastor preach on the Cross. Sometimes I think it's unfortunate the Cross presents such possibilities for dramatics. We get emotional sermons describing the awful suffering. I wonder what these preachers would have done if Christ had been executed in modern times—with a hypodermic, or in an electric chair. It would destroy all those vivid two-point sermons about the vertical and horizontal aspects and how Christ's arms are outstretched to enfold all those who kneel at the Cross.

Please don't misunderstand. I'm not being sacrilegious. But the power of Christ's death is not in the dramatics. In fact, Christ did not suffer there as many hours as the thieves did. The power of Christ's death was in his becoming sin for us, and ultimately in his resurrection and victory over death.

So the redemptive approach is not to make Christ's death a spectacle but to bring the significance of it to the unseeing. It is living in the victory of his resurrection.

This is what leadership is all about: raising people's level of maturity. We raise it by bringing first knowledge, then understanding, and eventually wisdom.

A Balanced Church Life

Another area where maturity demands an integrated, seamless understanding is the extent of our involvement in church functions. This involves both time and use of gifts.

No one can mature spiritually without worship. There is no way to be mature without having fellowship with Christian brothers and sisters, without having a good relationship with the church itself. The church is ordained of God, and if I want to be in the middle of God's activity, I must be involved in my local fellowship of believers.

Somebody asked me one summer when it was 102 degrees in Dallas, "Why do you go to church?" I sheepishly admitted that one August I had sat in church during a very predictable sermon and written an essay outline on that subject. The first reason was that Scripture commands it. The second was that I needed it at least once a week to position myself under the lordship of Christ.

He and I are not partners; we are not equals. I am subordinate. Sitting there in church each week, I recognize and renew the subordinate position.

But this truth needs to be balanced with another: It's not always healthy to go to church every time the doors are open.

I appreciate what Terry Fullam, Episcopal priest in Connecticut, said to one woman who was there for almost every activity: "You are here at church too much. If it keeps on, I'm going to suspect you have a lousy family relationship." As it turned out, he later discovered that was the case. Church had become an escape from the home.

Church should never become the equivalent of a country club, where some people go three nights a week just to get away.

Like anything else, church attendance, to be mature, must be homogenized with the rest of life. Some pastors try to increase church involvement by getting people to decrease their involvement in other things. They set up a war: The spiritual segment fights the other segments of life. If people would cut down on time spent in PTA, on golf courses, or coaching Little League, they could come to church more often and put their time into the spiritual segment—or so goes the reasoning.

Unfortunately, that battle does not always lead to maturity. It certainly doesn't encourage godly people to take the gospel with them as they move throughout their world.

During Richard Halverson's long pastoral ministry, before he became chaplain of the United States Senate, he was known for visiting his people where *they* were. He would go to oil rigs, kitchens, car dealerships, nurseries, and executive suites. He had no agenda other than to visit and remind these people they were Christ's representatives in that place. This was his way to homogenize, to encourage maturity.

This approach requires a secure, unthreatened leader. Some church leaders are afraid to homogenize the spiritual because they fear losing their one area of control. Church functions are the one place where the pastor is in charge, and he wants to be able to identify how much of the people's lives he controls or contributes to.

That approach would be fine if our goal were simply to increase attention to church. But increasing the level of activity is not the goal; increasing the level of *maturity* is the goal.

Mature leaders understand that controlling more hours per week may not be a worthwhile goal. It may even conflict with beneficial family interests.

The Leader's Role

How do we lead people into maturity? The first step is to lead ourselves into maturity, partly through the personal disciplines, which we discussed in chapter 4. We may never reach complete maturity this side of heaven, but we certainly cannot lead others into maturity unless we are experiencing the maturing process and becoming more consistent, well balanced, and whole.

Beyond that, however, the leader's role is to help people see their entire life as an expression of their faith, to apply their Christianity to all the diverse areas of their lives.

Some young pastors are sure to ask, "How do I personally help that process? I'm trained in theology, and you're saying that to help people mature, I have to apply the faith to being a sheet metal worker, an auto mechanic, or a public school-teacher. I don't have any expertise in those fields. What can I do?"

It's a fair question, and my answer has two parts.

On one hand, the quickest way to appear a phony is to believe you can become a great varied resource for a large number of people at an early age. You can't. Young pastors are like young teachers who study tomorrow's lesson tonight, barely staying ahead of their students. Through skimming, they often collect superficial answers. Likewise, some young pastors try to counsel in areas where they have no experience. Only time, knowledge, and experience with people can provide the depth of necessary understanding.

On the other hand, even young pastors can point people to the appropriate resources. "You know, Joe is involved with that. It might be helpful for you to ask him what his experience has been." We can help develop maturity in the congregation primarily by taking advantage of the body's resources. Leaders don't have to be the only resource for guidance.

Personally, I'm impressed with churches that make use of their older in-house advisers. Recently my wife has been asked by three or four young mothers for advice on child raising. "How do you live through this stage?" Mary Alice does a marvelous job of quietly talking it through with them. By the end of the conversation, the young mothers realize they'll make it.

In business, we have staff advisers, consultants, and specialists we call upon for particular needs. If I were heading a church ministry, I would try to do the same. I'd publish a list of people with expertise they are willing to share—an experience bank. I wouldn't make them turn in reports on their activity; I'd simply make it known they are available to minister to those with questions.

Often when I'm teaching a large group, I'll say, "You can't believe how many problems are in this group. . . . But you know something else? You don't realize how many answers are in this group, either. You probably know the problems are here, but you don't know how many people here have gone through exactly what you're going through right now and have found a solution."

Wouldn't it be marvelous if we could stop the class and just match up the people who have the problems and those who have found answers?

That's one of the prime functions of leadership in developing a mature congregation. You make all the resources of Christianity and the body of Christ available to everybody. The leader becomes the chief networker, the facilitator, helping people turn to one another (and to himself in some cases), recognizing all the gifts and resources within the church. This also helps produce integrated, unsegmented Christians, because you're involved in all the diverse areas of life—work, education, art, family life, recreation—and people begin to see these are all part of Christian living.

The Test of Mature Leadership

How can you tell when a church is well led? Often by what happens when the leader is *not* there.

I attended First Evangelical Free Church in Fullerton, California, a few weeks ago on a Sunday when Charles Swindoll did not speak. I was impressed by the friendliness, the way people talked to each other. I saw people whose ministry seemed to be that of encouragement. They went around greeting people, passing out little compliments. The place was better for them being there. In a good organization, the ministry continues whether the leader is there or not. That, to me, is a sign of a maturing body—and a sign of good leadership.

I appreciate the ministry of Frank Tillapaugh, who has done a marvelous job emphasizing lay leadership at Bear Valley Baptist Church in Denver. He was asked one time, "How do you know when to take on a project?"

"Any time a legitimate need surfaces, and we have enough people willing to accept responsibility for it, our automatic response as a church is yes," he said. He is quick to recognize the ministries of lay leaders.

At a meeting with fifty church leaders, I was explaining the way Frank encourages people to develop their own ministries. Immediately one staff pastor said, "But how can you protect the church against that?" He missed the point entirely!

Another pastor wanted to know, "How can you keep control in a church that flexible?" It was obvious he felt the church should be run only by the professional staff.

Again, the purpose of the church is not to give pastors positions of responsibility. It is not to run well-organized programs for people. It is not to protect people from responsibility. The mission of the church, and therefore the purpose of church leadership, is to develop mature Christians.

Are people applying their faith to all areas of their lives? Are they creating opportunities to serve? To develop their own gifts? Would the ministry continue on without me?

If we can answer those questions in the affirmative, we are well on our way to successfully leading a congregation to maturity.

TWELVE

THE INVISIBLE SIDE OF LEADERSHIP

The most important thing in life is not to capitalize on our gains. Any fool can do that. The important thing is to profit from our losses.

Congregations sometimes judge leaders by "apparent success"—and we sometimes judge ourselves that way as well. But leadership is more than outward. To lead a congregation, we must recognize some intangible factors, both good and bad.

Let's start by identifying three false indicators of successful leadership.

1. *Succeeding at a private agenda.* When this happens, the leader progresses but the people don't. A pastor builds a large church, for example, in order to win a denominational post rather than to serve the people.

General Electric once learned that young eager beavers running branch or subsidiary operations would sometimes take short cuts that didn't show up until after they were promoted upward. They would cut maintenance expenditures, for example, and throw the money into the profit column. That made them look extremely good. The next fellow would come along, however, and find a lot of overdue maintenance waiting for him. GE decided to add a section to its evaluation procedure for executives: What effect has this person had on the *future* of the operation?

In the same way, the pastor who takes too many outside speaking engagements is pursuing a private agenda. The person who wants to pray at every football game or social event, to be continually seen with the right people, looks like a leader—but is he? He may become a prominent person but not be leading the church to help people mature or to reach the lost. It's a private agenda.

2. Measuring success by the competition. Why do we seldom refer to the pastor of a small church as a "leader"? Because we've adopted a competition mode of thinking.

Doing better than other people doesn't mean we're successful. We still might not be doing anything close to what we ought to be doing. The essence of leadership is progress toward our spiritual goal, not competition.

But it's easy to get diverted. In fact, some who are renowned for leading congregations are really immunizing the people against real responsibilities. I sincerely believe pastors of many large churches have learned how to make the irresponsible comfortable. For my personal edification, I once made a list of the ways it can be done. For example, talking only about the total budget, seldom about per capita giving. That way, a pastor can emphasize the seven- or even eight-figure sum— and the people are impressed because the budget is usually larger than last year. But on an individual basis, they may be doing far less than a tithe, perhaps *less* per capita than the year before. To me, that's not leading people to responsible giving.

When there's lots of hype and little effort required, people will gather. True leaders, however, help people assume responsibility, not avoid it.

3. Popularity. The fact that people feel warmly toward a pastor doesn't mean he's a good leader at all. It simply means he has a likable personality. A lot of times it's more important to get the job done than to be liked.

I got some criticism once from my Sunday school teaching, so I had my secretary type up a card with a quote from Martin Luther: "I find it impossible to avoid offending guilty men, for there is no way of avoiding it but by our silence or their patience; and silent we cannot be because of God's command, and patient they cannot be because of their guilt." Every Christian leader ought to put that in a frame. There's no way to keep the hit dog from hollering. The trick for a Christian is to continue to love that hollering dog.

What Derails Leaders

Impressive-looking leaders can veer into the ditch for a couple of reasons:

• *They were steered by their ego.* This kind of person reminds me of the inspector in the underwear commercial: "It isn't Hanes until I say it's Hanes." That was pretty much the style of one association president I knew, who when asked for the basis of a certain decision, replied, "My word." This man was elected to twenty-seven one-year terms in a row, and he eventually got to thinking he was God. Then came his downfall.

I saw the leader of a major church fail not long ago. His word had gotten to be law. If he said it, you didn't argue with it. In the end, all moral ground gave way.

A lot of leaders start out humbly, with right purposes, but get diverted into ego trips. Many electronic preachers start out sincere as they can be, but often the ratings catch their eye, and they become showmen.

• *They became discouraged.* This is an opposite reason for derailment, and a more common one. Some of us don't have enough success to get on an ego trip. The train isn't rolling that fast.

But we do get sidetracked by small failures. We somehow can't quite muster the second and third effort to keep trying again. Leadership means plugging away until the break-through comes. My mother, in the midst of raising five boys on a preacher's salary, used to repeat and repeat: "Let us not be weary in well doing: for in due season we shall reap, if we faint not" (Gal. 6:9). That's a great verse for the heart of any leader.

Staying on Track

Bill Glass, All-Pro football player of the 1960s, said he was never on a winning team that didn't have high morale. But the morale came from winning; winning did not come from the morale. "That's what people who are not in leadership don't understand," he said.

It's important for a leader to generate some progress—some "wins"—to show people. Browbeating them with their failures is a poor way to motivate. People need to see success, to catch a feeling of progress.

No matter what the circumstances, there is always some kind of progress to be made. A congregation of 250 farmers will make progress different from a city church's. But progress is possible. The leader finds out what that is and leads in that direction. It may not be dramatic. But as long as he's making progress, he's leading.

Charles Pitts, the man whose company built the Toronto subway, told me, "When you ride up to a site and find fifty or a hundred people standing there waiting for the boss to make a decision, you don't call a committee meeting. You get them busy immediately. If you don't know exactly what to do, you at least get them doing something that won't hurt. People have got to feel the boss knows what ought to be done."

A leader simply must have the confidence to lead. You can't afford to get confused in front of your people. If you want to be confused, do it at home! Confusion, like prayer, is best in a closet.

Every leader also needs to understand that early sacrifices have to be made in order to earn a place in leadership. When you are young, you can't set out to be both a Rubenstein and a baseball star. You have to pay the price of preparation, both formally and informally. A lot of people come out of seminary thinking they're automatic leaders. No, they're *candidates* for leadership.

A friend of mine, Glenn Baldwin, upon selling his very

successful investment company, was asked the secret of his success.

"Well," he said, "back when I started twenty-two years ago, I worked very hard and had a good year. Twenty-one years ago, I worked hard and had my second good year. Then twenty years ago, I worked hard and had my third good year. . . . The secret of my success was twenty-two consecutive 'good years.' "

The questioner replied, "Is that all? Wasn't there some secret?"

"There was no secret, no trick," Glenn said. "I just put one good year on top of another."

People these days will read *In Search of Excellence* and think they're going to find some secret formula. More than any secret techniques, the quality companies all have quality leadership.

Now I will admit the magnitude of a leader's success is not always determined by the person or his qualities. Often, the times bring special opportunities. Abraham Lincoln would never have been known as perhaps our greatest president without the Civil War. Winston Churchill's career was fading into insignificance until the Second World War came, and Britain needed a man of his talent.

But this is only one factor. Far more is decided by how intelligently we work. We cannot dictate the times, but as Mordecai said to Esther, "Who knows but that you have come to royal position for such a time as this?" We are responsible for the situation into which we have been placed.

As the sign my wife hung over the washing machine says, "Bloom where you are planted."

An Eye on the Destination

A leader should never try to lead without first being captivated by a vision. Paul never lost the vision of his divine appointment to be an apostle to the Gentiles.

Intensity must always have focus, of course. If you are intense about the wrong things, people will lose respect and think you are a neurotic or religious fanatic. The vision must always be of the possible. It's very romantic to say, as some do, "Never attempt anything that isn't too big for you, so you'll be sure God has to do it." How much better to tackle those things he gives that are at hand and doable.

Seldom does an unknown person win an Olympic gold medal. Seldom does a no-name catapult into a place of leadership. In fact, the Scripture says not to use a novice. We disobey that sometimes by taking a person who's been successful in one field and moving him into the spiritual arena. Just because someone's led a business or made money does not mean he's a spiritual leader. Leaders are grown; they accrete. Leadership requires experience and emotional control. It demands the ability to persuade, and the ability to solve problems.

The vision we pursue must be worthy. It must make the effort seem like a good investment. Those asked to do the work must say, "What I'm doing is worth the cost." This is one weakness in the Soviet system right now. People don't see anything happening that's worthy of their effort.

When Torrey Johnson, a young pastor of a small Chicago church, founded Youth for Christ back in the 1940s, he wasn't just chasing numbers. He saw an opportunity to do something for soldiers hanging out on the street on Saturday night. From that movement has come some of evangelicalism's greatest leaders. At the 1974 Lausanne Congress on World Evangelization, there was a gathering of former YFCers, and the room turned out to contain much of the leadership of the evangelical world. That's what can happen when you pursue a worthy vision.

Leadership is the ability to see beyond the odds—to see how you can *change* the odds. If you don't see that, you are asking for failure.

The goal may not be reached in your lifetime. But as Lincoln said, "I would rather fail in a cause that will ultimately succeed than succeed in a cause that will ultimately fail." Sometimes we leaders have to realize we are laying foundations—which always take shape much more slowly than superstructures. We can't get dissatisfied with the slow work of the diggings and pilings just because the person who will do the super-structure will appear to be doing so much more.

Leadership requires a certain patience. Generally our ego is the overlord of our patience, but in leadership it must be subservient. Six times around the walls of Jericho wasn't enough to make them fall. In the same way, a few years later it took Gideon quite a while to find his three hundred core men.

We don't lead masses except in entertainment, or at best moving them by short-term enthusiasm. On the other hand, *developing* people takes time. But it also has much more long-lasting effects. We need to remember we are serving the God of eternity.

Knowing What People Need

Leaders do not usually know, through intuition, what direction people need to be led. Most effective leaders pick up cues from their people's needs.

In the business world, Ted Levitt described the difference between sales and marketing. If you're oriented to selling, you start by deciding to manufacture a product—say, baby carriages—and you get the sales force to go out and sell them. In marketing, you go out and find what customers would like to buy; *then* you make that product. You start near the end of the process and work backwards.

Proctor and Gamble, for example, is a marketing company. Being a chemical company, they can make soap or toothpaste any way they want. But they went out and asked consumers, "What do *you* want?" Well, people said they'd like something to stop cavities. That sounded rather far-fetched at first, but before long we had flouride in the toothpaste, and our dental bills went down.

The church is a combination of sales and marketing. The

gospel is fixed, but not the emphasis. If you read Paul's letters, he spent much of the space dealing with what his readers wanted to talk about. They had written him with questions, and he was answering them. He always included the gospel, but he applied it to their specific needs.

If I said to a group of preachers, "Give people what they want," many would see it as a prostitution of the gospel. But the gospel is so broad. Yes, we all believe the Scripture provides answers to problems, but we'll get people much more involved if, like Paul, we talk about what their problems are. Too many say, "Well, I think the people ought to know Romans, or the Decalogue, or the miracles." Is that what they sense a *need* to know?

As long as you are dedicated to bringing scriptural principles to bear on people's problems, you're a marketer. You're helping people with the problems they have by applying "the mysteries of God," as my friend Ray Stedman would put it.

We've learned in industry that most people will not learn anything they are not going to use shortly. Very few are intellectually curious, wanting to learn for learning's sake. If you tell somebody how to get to a certain stadium, he'll probably forget—unless he wants to go to the stadium. If somebody stops you and says, "How do I get to the stadium?" you can be sure he's going to listen very well.

Somebody was raving to me recently about a certain television preacher. I said, "Is he good?"

"Oh, he's wonderful."

"What makes him a good preacher?" I asked.

She answered, "When you get through listening to him, you'd think he's been in your living room all week. He knows where you are."

Interior Leadership

While leaders at the top are evident and visible, leadership must be exerted all through an organization. That's why Jethro told Moses to divide up the responsibility and the authority. Moses didn't keep it all to himself.

In any well-run organization, a whole group of leaders and developing leaders are coming up. Leaders cannot operate without help. That is why, at another time, Moses needed to have his arms held up. He knew what he wanted to accomplish. But he was physically incapable by himself.

I know a preacher right now who's tearing a church apart because he's saying to people, "Look, we're going to succeed whether you come with us or not. Stay under the stairs if you want. We don't need you—you need us." That's not good leadership.

Leadership is more than personality; it's character. The accomplishment of a goal requires synergy. For each goal is part of a larger goal, thereby developing momentum. You don't get diverted; you stick with your master plan. The followers then enjoy the fruits of their labor. There are celebration times, when you say, "Hey, we've done well. I appreciate you; your hard work is recognized."

Good leadership brings out the best in people; it makes more of any individual than he would have been had he not followed. Winning makes the organization willing to pay the price of discipline. And unless you make people conscious of winning, discipline becomes very odious. This has been a weakness of puritanical Christianity.

One of the toughest bandmasters I ever knew was Willy Fenten, a German who produced a championship high school band year after year. I can still hear him hollering at one trumpet player, "You can't play like that and play in this band! This is a championship band." Fenten didn't emphasize his own personal displeasure. He emphasized the student's contribution to the organization, and the quality of the organization. Therein lies a significant difference.

Is It Worth It?

When Harold Hook was voted "CEO of the Year" by Texas A&M, he outlined in his acceptance speech what he called three important questions for leaders:

1. *Am I enjoying what I am doing?*
2. *Am I happy with where I'm going?*
3. *Am I satisfied with what I'm becoming?*

I was impressed with that and sent it along to some friends of mine, including a young man, who three days later called me. We had an interesting conversation.

"Fred, you're going to think I've gone off my rocker."

"Why?"

"I just liquidated my investments."

That stopped me for sure. I said, "Do you know something about the stock market I don't—like, a crash?"

"No."

"Were you losing?"

"No, I was making money."

"Did you need the money?"

"No."

"Then why'd you do that?"

He said, "Fred, I'm sick and tired of grabbing *The Wall Street Journal* first thing every morning. That is not the object of my life. And when I read that thing you sent about 'Am I satisfied with what I'm becoming?' I said no. I'm becoming too involved in my investments. So I liquidated them today."

I said, "You didn't do a silly thing. You simply looked at your priority list and took action. You did well."

I saw him three days later. "How do you feel now?" I asked.

"I feel exactly like I did when I quit smoking," he said. "I'm free."

It is important that the act of leading make us become what we want to become. This way we do not end up hollow, having our insides eaten away by success. Paul said he had run the race and finished the course; he was satisfied with his leadership. That, in the end, should be the product of any leader's life.

THIRTEEN

THE REWARDS
OF LEADERSHIP

In every significant event, there has been a bold leader, an object or purpose, and an adversary.

Leadership is most often the means God chooses to fulfill his purpose. When God wants something done, he turns to an individual—Moses, Paul, Luther, Wilberforce, Moody, Mother Teresa—name them. Great things rarely get done by consensus. According to the organizational axiom, "Power is always personal."

Interestingly, the persons God picks as leaders aren't always the ones we would have picked. His leaders would not always have been elected. In a democracy, I doubt the apostle Paul would have made it. Leaders must be willing to be lonely.

Albert Schweitzer, for instance, gave up a prosperous musical, medical, and academic career in an affluent society to obey the verse of Scripture "If any man have not the Spirit of Christ, he is none of his." He went to the Congo and spent the rest of his life developing a hospital at Lambaréné. Norman Cousins tells the story of visiting him, and as the canoe neared shore, Schweitzer waded out to meet him. Then he grabbed Cousins's luggage and started carrying it up the hill. Cousins, much younger than Schweitzer, protested that he could carry his own bag.

Schweitzer turned and said, "Young man, in Lambaréné I am the leader, and I hope I will not find you difficult."

Schweitzer, no doubt, faced days of loneliness. But leaders are sustained by knowing that they are part of something greater than themselves.

God works through leaders who accept the responsibility. Often leading is hard work, but it also awards some profound benefits. I often say, "If the president and the janitor drew the same pay, I'd still want to be the president." What are some of these substantial benefits of being a leader?

Personal Development

One of the high points of the last couple of years for me was meeting with Ray Stedman and about fifteen top preachers in the United States to discuss how to encourage effective expository preaching.

During one lunch, I was moved most deeply. Stephen Olford said, "My brothers, I am weary of celebrity religion. I have had my share of recognition, but if when I die my family doesn't say, 'There was something of the Spirit of the Lord in that man,' I have failed." A solid, spontaneous amen rose around that table.

These leaders had developed the process that turns knowledge into wisdom. I realized again that the greatest leaders do not try to impress, but their commitment to the Lord and their leadership positions combines to develop maturity. Leadership requires maturity; it also helps to produce it. This is a reward of leadership.

For those who have the talent to lead, leadership is a great self-fulfillment. I don't know of anything more frustrating than for such a person not to have the opportunity to lead. Can you imagine the frustration of a Rubenstein if he never touched a Steinway?

Leaders come to the satisfaction, if they've used their talents well, of knowing they have run the race, finished the course, and become what they ought to have become. They will be commended by the Lord as much for their character as their specific accomplishments.

Developing Persons

Beyond self-fulfillment, leadership offers a chance to see others fulfilled. Leaders help people see what they ought to be and accomplish what they ought to accomplish. This is why vision is so important. Leaders have that ability to see what others can't see and to believe, before others believe, that it can be accomplished.

Many people differ in their evaluation of my friend Robert Schuller—but you have to admit he has supreme vision. You have to marvel that a young man preaching in a drive-in theater with a portable organ played by his wife could envision the Crystal Cathedral and raise it into reality. Without his leadership, it would never have happened. He gave people that great sense of accomplishment, of fulfillment, being part of something significant. Like baseball player Bobby Richardson once said, "When you put on those Yankee pinstripes, you play better." In a sense, that's what leadership does. It helps people accomplish what they would not have accomplished otherwise.

I will always be indebted to Maxey Jarman. He was my leader for the forty-three years I worked for him and with him. I'll never lose the feeling of accomplishment, the valuable experiences, the lessons I learned from him. I am a better man, better equipped to help others, for the years I spent with him. That's a normal feeling followers have toward a capable leader. I hope I've passed that experience on to those responsible to me.

Productive, Not Happy

I wrote myself a note the other day criticizing my compulsion to be productive. At my age, why can't I just be happy with who I am, with no concern about my productivity?

As I was writing how much better it is to be happy than productive, however, I realized that's impossible for a leader. Happiness and productivity are concomitant for a leader.

The more I thought about it, I saw that a desire to be happy and content with yourself is basically selfish. Perhaps not an evil selfishness, but certainly self-oriented. A desire to be productive, however, is not selfish. It is a desire to do something of value in which others share.

To me, much of the reward of leadership is simply the sense of being productive, producing something through others and for others that would not have been produced if the effort had not been expended.

By the time I finished my note, I had concluded, "Leaders would rather be productive than happy." (Sometimes writing, like preaching, most affects the one doing it.)

Ironically, productivity is not the same as doing. Leaders are often most productive when they are not *doing*. Sometimes their most significant work is instilling vision and excitement in others, having thoughts worth passing on—which often happens best in seemingly casual settings.

Whenever I teach a class, for instance, I feel it's my responsibility to communicate my availability to help people. I seldom say it directly, but the message gets across. I might slip in a comment such as "I had a wonderful time last week. Somebody called me, and we chatted for an hour over the phone about a decision he had to make." Or, "I talked with a confused woman today who needed my ancient experience." Well, those are invitations. Or perhaps I'll mention a particular issue and say, "I'd love to explore this topic in depth with you sometime."

Recently a doctor and his wife called and said, "Were you serious when you said you were willing to talk about this?"

"Yes I was," I said. So they invited Mary Alice and me to their home for dinner.

When we got there, we were delighted to meet three other couples they'd asked to join the conversation. They all had notebooks and pencils, and we had a serious, productive discussion. I thoroughly enjoyed it.

Like the blessing of a teacher who comes across a genuine student, leaders sometimes find other individuals who share their passion. You don't find many people like that, but when you do, it is a rich reward.

A Vicarious Thrill

Some leaders are visible and receive acclaim for their work. Often, however, leaders find their best reward within. Few leaders can stay motivated unless they've learned to appreciate the vicarious thrill of seeing others succeed.

Conversely, some of the greatest leaders I've known have also had friends who vicariously shared their accomplishment—those quiet people who pray fervently with Billy Graham. I heard about one man who came to see Mark Hatfield when he was governor of Oregon. The man said, "Governor, I haven't anything to ask. I simply want to pray with you." He got down beside the desk and prayed with the governor.

A worthy goal for an aging leader is to learn to give up the power, the day-to-day responsibility, and become a shepherd of shepherds. The point is not to usurp positions but to mentor younger people and simply say, "I'm available." The task is not to impose advice (because advice imposed is not advice but an order), but to suggest options and help clarify the other person's thinking.

I thoroughly enjoy working with younger people. I love to throw these young tigers some meat and watch them tear into it. I would imagine any leader must have that same sense of enjoying watching others develop and do well.

"God's Person in God's Place"

Finally, and perhaps most importantly, leaders are rewarded by knowing they are where God wants them . . . with a task great or small.

Mother Teresa leads in a quiet way. She is not overcome that she is making hardly a dent in the problem of poverty and suffering in India. She simply remains faithful. The hundreds she touches can't compare to the thousands who are dying, but she isn't discouraged. Her one candle is better than total darkness. She is fulfilling her calling.

Many years ago, my friend Torrey Johnson sent me his picture, inscribed with a message. I never felt I could hang it on my wall, but I occasionally get it out of the closet to read the inscription:

"To God's man in God's place."

On rare occasions I've had the feeling I was God's man in God's place. That's the greatest reward of leadership. Not that I have accomplished so much as a leader, but that what I have accomplished has sometimes been worthy and blessed by God.